365 Thank Yous

365
Thank Yous

THE YEAR A SIMPLE ACT
OF DAILY GRATITUDE
CHANGED MY LIFE

John Kralik

ⒽⓎⓅⒺⓇⒾⓄⓃ

NEW YORK

"Junk"
Copyright 1970 Sony/ATV Music Publishing LLC. All rights
administered by Sony/ATV Music Publishing LLC, 8 Music Square West,
Nashville, TN 37203. All rights reserved. Used by permission.

Library of Congress Cataloging-in-Publication Data

Kralik, John.
    365 thank yous : the year a simple act of daily gratitude changed my life / John Kralik.
        p.   cm.
    Includes bibliographical references.
    ISBN 978-1-4013-2405-6
    1. Kralik, John.   2. Gratitude.   3. Thank-you notes.   I. Title.   II. Title:
Three hundred and sixty-five thank yous.
    CT275.K845A3 2010
    179'.9—dc22

2010031228

Hyperion books are available for special promotions and premiums. For details
contact the HarperCollins Special Markets Department in the New York office at
212-207-7528, fax 212-207-7222, or e-mail spsales@harpercollins.com.

Design by Jennifer Daddio/Bookmark Design & Media Inc.

FIRST EDITION

10   9   8   7   6   5   4   3   2   1

To my children . . . and for Grace

CONTENTS

I. The Lowest Day   *1*

2. A Walk in the Mountains   *11*

3. New Year's Mail   *18*

4. My First Thank-You Note   *22*

5. How Are You?   *35*

6. Reading *Pollyanna* in Sierra Madre; or, Life
as a Series of Fortunate Events   *48*

7. An End of Winter   *64*

8. Thank You for Paying Your Bills   *66*

9. Thank the Starbucks Guy   *77*

10. Mediation   *92*

11. Birthday Cards   *96*

12. *Doctor Hudson's Secret Journal*   *108*

13. Extreme Thank Yous   *125*

14. The Unopened File   *134*

15. Father's Day   *138*

16. A "Business" Trip to Beijing   *140*

17. Economic Meltdown on Lake Avenue   *144*

18. Heartbreak   *151*

19. The Stock Market Crashes . . . into Thanksgiving   *162*

20. Running with Friends   *169*

21. In Training   *179*

22. December, the Movie and the Reality; or,
It's a Wonderful Life   *185*

23. A Better Man   *190*

24. A House, a Dream Job, Grace, and a Sandwich
Wrapped in Waxed Paper; or, What I Wanted   *201*

Epilogue: A Tie   *211*

Appendix I: How to Write Thank-You Notes   213

Appendix II: A Statement of Ideals   219

Acknowledgments   223

365 Thank Yous

CHAPTER I

The Lowest Day

On December 22, 2007, I felt my life was at an irreversible personal nadir. My law firm was losing money and losing its lease. I was going through a difficult divorce, was completely out of funds, and was living in a small, stuffy apartment where I often slept on the floor under an ancient air conditioner. My sons had grown distant from me. A horrible year was ending, with promises that things would soon be even worse.

I still remember that lowest day. On my way to work that morning, I got a call from my friend Bob, who had gone to law school with me in Michigan thirty years before.

Bob asked how I was doing. This was a mistake. Poor Bob. "Not good" is what I said, and my tone was desperate and bitter. I no longer had the ability to pretend that everything was "fine." Bob asked if I wanted to go to breakfast. Another mistake.

Later, he would tell me he had never seen me this upset.

That morning, Pasadena was entering its famous, seductive New Year's beauty. With businesses and schools closed for the holidays, the smog clears from the mountains, revealing, just four miles up Lake Avenue from where I stood, the fresh winter brush of the San Gabriel foothills, each ridge a different shade of misty gray in the soft morning light. But I wasn't in those gorgeous foothills. I was meeting Bob at a dingy coffee house near the dust and the vagrants of Pasadena's downtown center. Although the chain restaurant was Bob's choice, I couldn't afford to eat anyplace nicer; I couldn't even afford to eat at this place.

The man Bob saw across the chipped Formica table was fifty-two years old, forty pounds overweight, pasty, and tired, with a terrified sadness in his eyes. After twenty-eight years of work as a lawyer, I had little more to show than I'd had when I started—and the little I did have was in jeopardy.

Perhaps because I did not need to be in court that morning and hadn't steeled myself for court, my usual stoicism about my situation had broken down. I was letting my true feelings show.

As I explained to Bob, I had worked harder than ever at being a good lawyer in 2007. The results were in. I was a failure.

First, a pair of clients for whom I had recovered more than a million dollars that year had stopped paying my bills. When I brought this to their attention, one of them started writing me e-mails with the subject heading "Your 'Bills.'" Together, they owed me $170,000, which I needed to make my end-of-year payroll and pay Christmas bonuses, and maybe have something left over for myself. Although they could not agree on much else, these clients decided to work together on a plan that could eliminate their attorneys' fees. They jointly ordered the money I had recovered transferred to Texas, where I could not lien it to pay my bills.

Then there was the case of the sweet woman who had asked me to sue a gentleman she believed was helping her brother hide money from her. After my client gave up the case, it became apparent she'd had a brief affair with the defendant before suing him. Something about the way the affair ended, combined with getting sued, left this defendant unsatisfied with a mere dismissal. So he sued me for having taken on her case against him.

When I sat down to breakfast with Bob, I had just paid a retainer to the lawyers who would defend me and had begun the process of going through every document, every e-mail, and every pleading in the case to formulate my defense. The suit against me was a plain example of how legal proceedings can become a circle of hatred, in which each vicious legal move is countered by an even more malevolent one, until everyone is out of money. In my darkest moments, I worried that my client's ex-suitor and his relentless desire for revenge would not only leave me completely out of money but would call my practice into question, effectively ending my career as a lawyer.

Seven years before, I had started my small law practice idealistically. Like some wannabe legal Jerry Maguire, I had set forth my ideals in a mission statement, "The Statement of Ideals," which I shared with my associates and even posted on the wall and on my Web site. For example, I promised to be "true to our beliefs in right and wrong, both as lawyers and as human beings."

I signed clients up at low rates commemorated in simple, one-page retainer agreements, because I wanted to avoid the page after page of legal mumbo jumbo that most lawyers use to cover their backsides. My rates were low, because I worried about the effect of my bills on my clients. I wanted to "do no harm," which my father, a surgeon, had always preached to me as the foundation of his ethics. Unlike a doctor's, a lawyer's treatment does often, in Hippocrates' words, "injure or wrong" a client. I wanted to help people before my bill became their biggest problem, and I became the principal person harming them.

But during 2007 I learned, in a painful way, that such idealism had serious limitations as a business model.

I tried to be logical about what would happen next. It seemed insane to keep trying to do what I had been doing, but I could not see a way out, with all my clients and my employees depending on my willingness to proceed. I had counted on the clients who owed me the $170,000, and I felt too embarrassed to tell my employees now, just three days before Christmas, that there would be no money for year-end bonuses. Bob wondered why I was thinking of bonuses; why, with all my other problems, was it even on my mind?

Throughout the year, we had been trying to renew the lease on our office space, but then the building went up for sale and for months we had no landlord from whom to seek a new lease. Then, at the beginning of December, a new owner bought the building, and his first decision was to end our tenancy—unless we wanted to accept an above-market rent. When we balked, he asked us to leave as soon as possible. We now needed about $25,000 in cash if we wanted to sign a lease for comparable space in another building.

When you run a small law practice, much of what comes in also goes out—to rent, employees, insurance, and the other expenses of running the business. What's left at the end is your salary, so to speak. For me, for 2007, this "salary" was going to be nothing. In fact, it was less than nothing: I had lost $12,652. Clients had failed to pay nearly

$400,000 in bills. One client paid in toys worth an eighth of his bill. And he was one of the good ones! My last vacation had been in 2003. I had worked sixty hours a week all year, without a break—for less than nothing, it turned out.

I had accomplished a tour de force of failure.

Aside from producing no measurable compensation, my work and my role in the world that it represented had become detestable to me. I had wanted to help people as an attorney, but too often I was still just the vehicle whereby clients conveyed hatred, sought retribution, and inflicted pain on their fellow men and women. Some lawyers love the fight and never weary of it. I was not one of those lawyers. To me, the work was too often best done when I got in touch with my inner evil core. And I didn't want to be in better touch with my inner evil core.

My personal life provided no respite from the seeming financial failure of my practice. Four years before, my perhaps too relentless pursuit of law practice "ideals" had helped cause a separation from my second wife. After the separation, she had remained in our house, and I had moved into one of the nicer new apartments in town. Now that my money was running out, I was living in a small, cheap, poorly ventilated apartment that became an intolerable oven in the summer and cost hundreds of extra dollars in the winter because of inefficient electric heaters. Several nights each week, my seven-year-old daughter lived with me in this plaster box. In the summer, she and I slept on a plastic inflatable mattress in the living room under the loud, aging air conditioner, which provided a small pocket of coolness, as long as we lay on the floor directly underneath it.

By the beginning of 2007, after more than three years apart, I had thought my second wife and I at least had agreed we could not get back together. Yet by December 22, after more than a year of negotiation, we had no separation agreement, not even regarding custody of our daughter.

In addition to my daughter, I have two sons from my first marriage. On December 22, 2007, they were twenty-six and twenty-two. During the previous year, my older son had become largely self-sufficient, though there were still occasional cash-flow crises, and the tension from past calamities of this sort had left us distant. "Loans" had often turned into cash infusions. Sometimes clubbing and skiing had seemed to me to take precedence over gainful employment. Meanwhile, my younger son was still finding his way and required financial help not only with tuition and rent, but with his car, car insurance, parking and moving violations, and food.

In sum? My business was losing money, losing cases, and losing its lease. I was paying mortgages or rent for three households—my second wife's, my younger son's, and my own—when I couldn't afford one. My savings were exhausted. I stood to lose most of what I had earned since my first divorce in a second divorce. I was worried that I might also lose my daughter.

As the year progressed, there had been days when I was so preoccupied with my problems that I walked into the street without checking for a WALK sign. When a car missed me with a honk of the horn, I wondered whether everything might have worked out better had I been hit. I started to envy people who had heart attacks. I did not want to die exactly, but I began to think about the peace I could get in a hospital room, recovering from an accident or a heart attack. The responsibilities of my work would no longer intrude. For just a while, the depressing events might slow. Perhaps I could have a day, just twenty-four hours in a row, when I didn't have to work. When I shared this with Bob, he started to really worry. This was either too scary or so downright pathetic that it embarrassed Bob to hear it. "Come on, John, it's not that bad," he said. He wanted me to return to my usual stoicism. But I couldn't.

So he asked about Grace.

I had recently begun a relationship with a young woman in her mid-thirties, whom I will call Grace. Most women of Grace's age saw only my pasty figure. For a while, though, Grace had looked at me in a way that made me remember I had eyes, and that they were blue, not gray like the rest of me. After I met her, I had even bought a pair of contacts, flattered by the notion someone had noticed the color of my eyes and wanted to see them. Being with Grace reawakened parts of me that had become dormant. It had been a long time since I had experienced the joy of spending an evening out with a person who really seemed to love me. Seeing Grace, once a week at least, had seemed to stop the depression for a time. Bob had met Grace and felt I was pretty damn lucky to have another chance at love at my age. He assumed that by mentioning her he might break my mood.

But Grace had broken up with me the night before. We had been out to dinner and when she asked about my plans for Christmas, I had been vague. I had thought I needed to be vague. I was still trying to make plans with my wife that would allow my daughter to be with me for some portion of that day. After I knew those plans, I needed to make arrangements to see my sons. After I had these arrangements in place, I tried to explain, Grace and I could make plans. Grace concluded that this made her too low in my order of priorities. "I can't do this," she said, and asked to go home.

When I dropped her off, she insisted on walking up the driveway alone. I called up the darkened path, telling her I would be waiting if she changed her mind. I asked if, even if she didn't ever want to go out with me again, would she at least get together with me to exchange Christmas gifts? "I don't want a Christmas present from you," she called back. And with that, the only door in my life that seemed to offer hope closed.

What could I offer her, anyway? I was broke, I worked almost all the time, and I spent the remaining time trying to maintain contact with and take care of my children. There was no getting around the fact I was not available to Grace in the way she deserved. As she put it, "I want someone like you, just someone who's available."

It had not been a good year.

Bob reminded me that he had my cell phone number and he was going to use it—to check up on me. Neither of us knew then what would happen next, or that a year later, everything would have changed.

CHAPTER 2

A Walk in the Mountains

Before she broke up with me, Grace and I had planned to spend New Year's Day walking on the Echo Mountain trail that leads into Angeles National Forest above Pasadena. When the day came, I called her to see if she might still want to come. She had other plans. I would be starting the new year alone.

I decided to walk into the mountains anyway.

I took the three-mile hike above Pasadena on the Echo Mountain trail, which ends at the crumbled remains of an old hotel. Hot winds and constant mountain fires had burned down that hotel, again and again, and eventually, about seventy years ago, the owners had stopped rebuilding. Guests had reached the hotel by train on the Mount Lowe Railway, which was now defunct and had also since succumbed to the elements. Only corrupt and scattered remains of the track can be found. But spectacular views of the Los Angeles Basin stretch out below the crumbled stone bricks of the hotel's remains. On a clear day you can see all the way to the ocean.

On this semi-clear day, when I got to the old hotel site, I joined a host of New Year's early risers. (The AA crowd, I thought.) They were looking through binoculars, hoping to spy the Tournament of Roses Parade winding through the foggy streets of Pasadena below.

I could feel the distant rumblings of the parade, but I was in no mood for it, so I turned to walk deeper into the mountains. Eventually, the sounds of trombones and French horns faded. Longing to be completely alone, I meandered the back paths, pushing on until I was all by myself. Then I took a wrong turn, lost the path, and became completely lost.

I had no company that day but the inner voice that kept saying "loser." There was no one I wanted to ask on that walk who wanted to come with me. My desires and faults had left me solitary at middle age.

It was New Year's. There was new growth all around. It was time to make new resolutions. It was time to change.

I had felt this way before, of course; at fifty-two, I had a lot of unfulfilled New Year's resolutions.

But this year not only was I a loser at what I was doing, I also didn't want to do it anymore. I wanted to do something more meaningful with my life. I wanted to be more than just another lawyer slinging hatred for a living.

I had always wanted to write, I remembered. But thirty years ago, I had become a lawyer. Soon, I'd had a family to support; eventually, I had two families and a firm to support. There had never been time to write. A few months before my first child was born, I had packed up my writing neatly in files and put it away in a box. The box had fallen apart many times, but I had always replaced it. I had carried it from divorce to remarriage to divorce, from house to apartment to cheaper and cheaper apartments.

Now time was running out. I was older than the idol of my college years, Jack Kerouac, had been when he drank himself to death. I was just a bit younger than Hemingway had been when his muse so dimmed that he saw no point in living. As I struggled through the brush in search of a new path, I ran through ideas I'd had for writing projects over the years. This year, I thought, I should try to write something, and I should actually finish it. Yet even as this thought made its way through my mind, I knew how futile a thought it was. I had no time, no energy.

Still not finding the path, I began to slip and stumble in the rough. As I became more lost and tired, I began to despair of getting home before dark, much less finishing something I started in the new year. I imagined falling down into one of the ravines. If that happened, how would I survive the night?

Then I heard a voice: "Until you learn to be grateful for the things you have," it said, "you will not receive the things you want." I do not know who spoke to me. I could not explain this voice, or the words it said, which seemed to have no logical relation to the other thoughts in my head.

I was tired and frustrated. I sat down for a minute. The voice was loud. For me, the voice was loud enough that I thought it might be important, and that it might have an important message. I should not throw it away.

I sat there listening to my breath. The wheezing from my asthma subsided. As things grew quiet around me, I realized I had no choice but to get up, or I would still be sitting there at the end of the day. While I was not sure I wanted to go back, there was no point in staying. Feeling less exhausted, I pushed on.

The mountains in this area are not so complicated, and despite the drama in my head, a return to civilization was still available to an inexperienced hiker. Heading generally downward, I eventually found another trail, and made my way, slipping and sliding, to the old hotel. Sitting on the remnants of its concrete slab, I stared out at the vast, quiet expanse of Los Angeles. This is a perspective from which the most sordid distress of humanity can seem peaceful.

For some reason, at that moment I thought of my grandfather John Kralik Jr., a veteran of the First World War and a successful dealer in insurance, real estate, and the stock market. Perhaps he came to mind because when he was my age, my grandfather had already retired. When I knew him, he played golf and watched it on television. In the morning, he sat at his desk and checked stock prices. Perhaps I was dwelling on my own bitterness at the certainty that I would not be playing golf or checking stock prices anytime soon. I would be working for a long time, I thought, perhaps till the moment of death.

When I was about five, my grandfather gave me a silver dollar. My grandfather had twelve grandchildren at the time. Eventually he would have twenty-four, and he would often try to impress us. It was about 1960, and if you really wanted to wow a child in those days, you gave him or her a silver dollar. It seemed an impossibly large sum of money in a shiny, mysterious package. I didn't know how to spend it, and don't believe I ever did. Silver dollars doled out by my grandfather and other relatives in those days were confiscated by my parents, who did not trust us with them. Eventually, my mother put them in a bank account, and I believe they are still there today. Though the money would have made no difference to me, I should have paid more attention to the message that my grandfather delivered with it. He promised that if I wrote him a letter thanking him for this silver dollar, he would send me another one. That was the way thank-you letters worked, he told me.

I have only a few memories of my grandfather from this period of my childhood, but I remember well that on this occasion he was true to his word, and soon I had two silver dollars. Having experienced the truth of this principle, however, I failed to learn it. I never sent a second thank-you note for the second silver dollar. For some reason, I left it at that. It may be that I didn't need or want another silver dollar. After all, my mother would put it in the bank, and I would never see it. But I was blind to the real lesson he was trying to teach me. So I did not receive a third silver dollar.

A couple years before that walk in the mountains, as part of my pipe dream of a gentle, gallant law practice, I had fancied that I would be handwriting a lot of personal notes. My office manager had dutifully ordered some very nice personal stationery, several hundred notes and envelopes in a gentlemanly off-white. Soon we would be kicked out of our offices, and the return address on hundreds of unused envelopes would become obsolete.

Sitting on the concrete slab that is all that remains of the hotel at Echo Mountain, I listened to the voice, and then the following thoughts, first of my grandfather and his silver dollars, and then of the nearly useless envelopes. And I came up with an idea.

I would try to find one person to thank each day. One person to whom I would write a thank-you note. By the end of the year, I would have used up the stationery. I would have written 365 thank yous.

If my grandfather was right, I would have a lot more of what I was thankful for by the end of the year. If the voice was right, I would begin to get the things that I wanted. And if not, well, I had little more to lose.

I stood and began to walk down the mountain trail toward home. I had been in the mountains the entire day; I had walked nearly fifteen miles. I was exhausted and still had little hope, but I had figured out how I might go on. My only problem: Did I have anything to be grateful for? The way my life was going, I hardly thought so.

CHAPTER 3

New Year's Mail

By the end of the next day, I still had not identified anything that merited a handwritten thank-you note. Then I received one.

Given the tiny, broken-down place I was living, I'd had almost no one over and I'd given only a few people the address. Nothing of import ever came to me in that metal mailbox—only tangles of junk mail and the monstrous electric bill caused by the building's aging electric heaters. Nothing more.

Above the mailbox were the somewhat crazy notes written by our apartment manager, Mr. Robert. He wrote notes to the residents with stern accusations, as if those who disobeyed the rules of the apartment building were on a moral par with petty criminals.

He apparently did not know how to spell and his notes also featured random capital and small letters. Mechanized typeface cannot quite convey the effect. The notes looked something like this: "BIkEs and tOys LEFT oUT in WIkways are HzardouS to OHTers who LIVE HERE. THEy Will BE DISPOSED IF NOT REMOVED BY TMOR-ROW!!" These were, I thought, like the notes that are left by a serial killer who wants to make it impossible to analyze or track his handwriting. As there was never anything pleasant around or in my mailbox, I was often inclined to skip opening it altogether.

On this day I trudged up the stairs, weary from work, debating in my head whether to make the extra effort to check the mail or just to let it go to the end of the week. For some reason, I decided to check. And on this day there was something uncommon in the mailbox for me, something that I needed to read.

Despite the hopelessness of our December twenty-second conversation, Grace and I had spent a few hours together on Christmas Eve. She accepted my Christmas present, a watch, and offered me her own, cologne. Grace and I had made no decisions that night. We had said nothing about what would happen next. Maybe we would see each other again, maybe not.

My invitation to her to go walking with me in the mountains on New Year's Day had been my first attempt to figure out whether we might still see each other. When she said she had other plans, I assumed that those hours on Christmas Eve had been our last together. But on January 2, 2008, below Mr. Robert's latest threatening note, I discovered a simple, rectangular manila envelope in the midst of the junk mail. Opening the envelope, I found personal stationery of such extremely thick stock that it impressed me as if it were a scriptural tablet. The lines of writing were uncannily straight on the blank card; the perfectly neat printing had been crafted as if with the undiluted concentration of a star fourth grader, uncomplicated by the rush of events and tasks in an adult's life. The message was brief:

Dear John,

Thank you for the wonderful gifts you gave to me. I really enjoyed the time we shared together on Christmas Eve.
You are a joy, and I truly appreciate how special you make me feel!

Love,
Grace

To me, it was a perfect thank-you note. And it offered an important message even beyond letting me know that maybe Grace and I could still be together. Short, generous, and handwritten, it was a sign. I could not hope to duplicate the class of Grace's handwriting with my own scrawl, and I did not have the sense of line and space that would permit my writing to be so even, especially on unlined paper. But it seemed uncanny that Grace had written this note just before I'd determined thank-you notes to be my way out of despair. By thanking me for a Christmas present, she awakened me to something in my life, however small, for which I could be grateful. Her note was showing me the first step. And I was going to take it.

CHAPTER 4

My First
Thank-You Note

Like virtually everyone in America who was experiencing a good or bad year in 2007, I had received some Christmas presents. Perhaps not very many, and maybe not what I most wanted, but presents nevertheless. So I got started on my 365 thank-you notes by saying thank you for my Christmas presents.

I had never written thank-you notes for Christmas presents, and no one else I knew wrote them either. Why not? I wondered. Giving holiday presents is the central commercial and social event of the year. Even when finances and the economy are desperate, cultural pressure tells us we must rally, sacrifice, and go into debt to maintain the annual Christmas gift ritual. But where is the equivalent tradition of gratitude? Instead, after the gifts have been opened, we hurry back to the store to return them, hoping for a sale price on some longed-for item, a price now even lower than the pre-Christmas sales.

I assessed my Christmas presents of 2007. Most spectacularly, there was a coffee machine that made one cup of coffee at a time. It was my older son's gift. As I was taking stock, I considered not just each gift, but the message behind it. This gift was a message that my son had arrived, that he could give me a substantial object, and even give some thought to it. With this gift, he was saying that he knew something about me—that is, I'm a notorious caffeine freak.

And so, the first of 365 thank-you notes was written to my older son. It was January 3, about the date most of my past New Year's resolutions had been abandoned, as the bustle of another year of pleadings and motions, of bills and of billable hours, commenced. I was at my law office when I wrote the thank-you note to my son, but Grace's note kept me from giving in to work pressures before I started on my project, and so I wrote:

Dear Son,

Thanks so much for the astonishing single-cup coffee-maker. It's perfect for my office, where we can offer everyone a different kind of coffee with every cup. Moreover, I think my staff is a little tired of cleaning up the grounds, and this is a very clean process. Nevertheless, I'm toying with the idea of just keeping it for myself.

See you soon,
Dad

"See you soon." I looked at the page. Precisely what did I mean by that? When would I see him? When was the last time I had gone out of my way to spend time with him aside from a major holiday? Then I went to address the envelope, and I realized I didn't even know his address. He lived in an apartment on the west side of Los Angeles, but I did not know precisely where. I had never been to his apartment. I did not know what it looked like. He had a roommate I had never met. I believed he had a girlfriend. I had never met her either.

In writing this first note, I recognized that I had closed myself off from my son in a way that was inexcusable. I told myself I had done this in part because he needed to be more independent, but writing this first note made me realize I had gone too far. All children deserve to know that their parent is there for them, at all times. Any good parent would know exactly where a son or daughter was living, no matter what. As soon as I knew my son's address, I would find a way to go by there. Or so I told myself.

So I called him.

"Hey, I was just trying to get your address in my new system and wanted to make sure I had the zip code right."

"Oh, yeah. Hey, Dad, I wanted to stop by," he said. "Maybe we could go to lunch."

This was highly unusual. But perfect, I thought. I could assuage my guilt by taking him to lunch. He gave me his address, and I promptly used it to address the envelope of my first thank-you note.

Although I could have just placed the envelope in the office out-box, I asked my paralegal for a stamp, walked down two flights of stairs, and placed it in the mailbox.

The next day, January 4, my son came to my office. He is taller than I am. He has a gentle, funny nature that invites people into the zone beyond his good looks and muscular build. We are both quiet, however, and like my father and me, my son and I seldom address things directly, preferring to meander around the real subjects while discussing the Dodgers and the Lakers.

I suggested we go to a hamburger restaurant within walking distance of my office. We had gone to this kid-friendly place every week when he was younger, until he and his brother told me that they were sick of it. It had been years since then, however, and I thought he could probably endure this restaurant again. He was no kid, of course, but I was thinking there might be a little nostalgic value in this setting; I was also wondering whether I could afford to pay for lunch, and I thought it was possible to afford in this place.

We sat at a table made in the image of a surfboard, listened to beach music, and watched surfing videos, succumbing to the notion, which could have begun only in Los Angeles, that a meal must also include some form of entertainment. After ordering and some of our usual small talk, my son brought out a business letter–size envelope. It was bulging. He handed it across the surfboard, and, looking inside, I saw a pile of crisp one-hundred-dollar bills. Forty of them. "It's for the loan," he said.

I had forgotten about this "loan" and had no idea it had been this much money. I knew I had loaned him money, but I had long ago written it off on the imaginary ledger upon which it had been recorded. Yet here was a pile of money more impressive than all of my grandfather's silver dollars. This was instant karma.

When the overly cheerful teenage waitress in the Hawaiian T-shirt came by with the check, my son reached for it.

"I asked you to lunch," he said.

This was nearly as disorienting as the loan repayment. For once, I did not fight for the check. This was his moment, and I felt the need to let him have it. Another signal of change in the universe. We started talking about some real things. He told me how he was enjoying selling real estate, a job he had spent a year learning. I had financed some of this, and he was repaying the loan with his first big commission. I opened up to him about my difficulties in operating my own business. I explained how payroll and rent could consume the cash brought in by the few bills that were being paid on time. Nevertheless, I told him, it was fulfilling to be your own boss. He might want to consider it sometime.

Recovering my equilibrium after this strange and wondrous visit from my son, I realized I had another thank-you note to write. I had something important to say that had, to my disgrace, gone unsaid over lunch:

Dear Son,

Thank you for paying back the loan. It was a great day for me because, actually, I really needed the money at this moment. More important, it built trust in our relationship.

It showed me you were growing up as a man, and that you could be true to your word.

Love,
Dad

Of course, my son's coffeemaker was not my only Christmas present. There were also three books on tape, three ties, a DVD series, and a Starbucks card. Having spent thousands on Christmas presents for others, I was feeling like this was a pretty lean haul. Yet from the beginning, this project was not like other New Year's resolutions I had dreamed up. There was always something pushing me to the next step. Something would happen that would keep me going. Grace's thank-you note and my son's envelope of cash were the first of these events, but there would be more.

After my son's visit, I determined to recognize every single Christmas gift, whether I thought it was impressive or not.

As I began to write the other notes, I wondered once again how it was possible that I had never written notes to thank people for their Christmas gifts. Without the practice of writing notes, by February, one tie has blended into another, and who can remember who gave you the black one with the white dots? Even if you thought that it was a pretty special tie, you would have not only failed to thank the person who took the time and expense to make this gesture, but you would have entirely forgotten who it was. I decided to start tracking my thank-you notes, making a list of the people I thanked and the gifts they had given. Never again would I need to wonder who had given me a particular tie or book on tape.

Having completed thank-you notes for the material gifts I had received, I looked around for other, less material gifts to be thankful for. For example, my uncle Art, who was almost ninety, nearly blind, and grieving over the loss of his wife, my beautiful aunt Betty, had taken the time to write out his Christmas wishes and send them. So I wrote a thank-you note for this and other Christmas "gifts." Absent my new thank-you project, and the need to write a new thank-you note every day, I would not have appreciated, or even noticed, gifts in my life like these.

In the course of writing and tracking these initial notes with a list, I typed some of the text of the notes into my computer, where it encountered spell check. As a result, I discovered that I had been misspelling the word *grateful*—as *greatful*—for my entire life. Because I used the word so infrequently, no one had ever pointed this out. Yes, that's right: I had so seldom been grateful in my life that I didn't even know how to spell the word. I had been spelling it as if a greatful person was a person full of greatness, rather than a person full of gratitude. Once I knew how to spell the word, I started using it more, in the thank-you notes and elsewhere, finally expressing "gratitude" for things for which I should be grateful.

In the coming weeks, what began as a list to keep one Christmas tie differentiated from another developed into a spreadsheet. And after a few months, the spreadsheet grew in fields until it contained the names and addresses of the many people to whom I was grateful for material gifts or for acts of kindness. Once I'd added the name and address field, I recorded my son's address there. It took me a few months but I did visit his apartment, and when I set out to meet him, I did not need to ask where he lived.

My spreadsheet is now so unwieldy that it cannot be printed in any meaningful way. I hope to add to it for the rest of my life.

Before even the first of the notes had been received, writing them was making me realize I needed to change the way I viewed my life and the people in it. After all, some people had no Christmas presents at all. Some people had no children.

Before starting this project, I'm sure I had not written 365 thank-you notes in my entire lifetime. Now I planned to do that in a single year. Yes, things were really going to change. The immediacy of the loan repayment and lunch with my son, following, instantaneously, my first couple notes, created a euphoria. I'd received a mysterious spoken direction of greeting card quality on a walk through a foggy wooded area in the mountains. Perhaps I had found the Answer.

But then I calmed down. The truth was I had written only a few thank-you notes. And the first day I didn't have a Christmas present to write about, I couldn't think of anything else to be grateful for—with 355 notes to go. Look, I thought, maybe there were a few things for which I had been insufficiently grateful, but mostly my life sucked— and that was a pretty objective view. I might spend an entire year, $146 in postage, and countless hours writing notes, and where would I be? Would I still be euphoric after losing my business or after a few other losses? How long could I keep working this hard for less than nothing? If I died of a heart attack now, people would be wondering: What the hell happened to this guy? He was writing a lot of thank-you notes at the end for some reason. Must have been lonely.

Nevertheless, I decided to go on. After all, nothing bad had happened as a result of my Christmas-present thank-you notes. At least I had that to be thankful for.

On January 22, 2008, the actor Heath Ledger died in New York. In my view, Mr. Ledger had everything the modern world could give to a human being: good looks, wealth, talent, a beautiful family. He could live anywhere and everywhere, date anyone or everyone he wanted to. He had just delivered an Academy Award–worthy performance as the Joker in *The Dark Knight*. When I saw the movie later in the year, I felt it should have been called *The Joker*. But in January 2008, he had not been able to sleep without oxycodone, hydrocodone, diazepam, temazepam, alprazolam, and doxylamine. I couldn't sleep either, I thought, but as much as I felt my life sucked, I turned out to be luckier than Heath Ledger, who I would have otherwise thought the most blessed man on the face of the earth. We take gratitude where we can get it, I guess, because this sad bit of celebrity news reminded me I needed to be more thankful.

Not knowing where our relationship stood, I had waited to thank Grace for her present: my last Christmas-present thank you was my response to Grace, the source of my Christmas thank-you inspiration.

I called first. I wanted to get a sense of what to say. Should I be light and breezy? I brought up the impressive nature of her thank-you note.

"It's been a long time since I got a thank-you note for a Christmas present."

"Oh, that's my training from my mother," she said. "We were always told that a written thank you was important and required for any material gift. And we couldn't use the presents until the thank-you notes were written."

Grace's mother had once been queen of the Tournament of Roses. She had not only imposed this thank-you note writing duty on Grace but had shown her how to perform it with queenly elegance. She wrote beautiful handcrafted notes. They were internally contained works of art.

"Well, I really appreciated getting this note," I said to Grace.

"Of course," she said. "I love you."

From the first time she had said, "I love you," it had seemed impossible to me. It was always something of a shock, every time she said it. This time there was another message. Now I knew. It was not over. So I wrote:

Dear Grace,

Thank you for the cologne. I now have confidence that I can smell exactly the way you want me to. More important, thank you for taking the risk of loving me at a time of my life when few would have dared. Your love is a treasure I did not expect to find, and often feel I don't deserve. Thank you for this priceless gift.

Love,
John

Because I grew up in Ohio, Pennsylvania, and Michigan, Los Angeles's sunny winters always seem incongruous to me. They seem to cover over the process of decay and rebirth signified elsewhere by winter and spring. Here the process of decay is marked differently, by fire and flood and mudslide. In the midst of one of Los Angeles's curiously sunny winters, I had received a blessing to heal the hopelessness in my heart. And for once, I was responding with thanks.

CHAPTER 5

How Are You?

The second thank-you note I wrote as part of my project was for a Christmas present from my younger son. He had given me a book, a terrific book actually, Erik Larson's true-crime spellbinder about the 1893 Chicago World's Fair, *The Devil in the White City.* Then, on January 31, 2008, just like his older brother, my younger son handed me a repayment for a forgotten "loan." So I sent him a second thank-you note:

Dear Son,

   *Thank you for paying back the loan of $120. By being
true to your word you are building trust with others, and I
am glad to see that. I am also thankful for the other positive
changes in your life, your new job, the order you have brought
to your apartment. It is very gratifying for us to see.*

                                          Love,
                                          Dad

By February, so much instant karmic success had come
into my life from my Christmas thank-you notes that I was
encouraged to begin sending thank yous in the direction of
all of my problems, which is to say, in every direction. I even
began to send work-related thank-you notes—to clients
who paid; to clients who might pay; to friendly lawyers who
referred cases; to opposing lawyers who battled me in cases;
to court clerks, expert witnesses, real estate agents, loan bro-
kers, mediators, and others. If I could find gratitude in such
a sore spot of my existence as my unprofitable law practice,
that would be a miracle. But the surprising events in January
persuaded me to at least try to plant the seeds of appreciation everywhere. If I couldn't summon hope while writing
thank-you notes about my work life, I could at least summon

"Well, write them, then wait and see." Mostly, though, where work was concerned, I was living in a state of fear.

By February, most of my days still ended with my stomach tied up in knots of fear and anger. Fear over how my cases were turning out. Fear that my clients would not pay and that I would be unable to pay my employees' salaries and health insurance. Fear that I couldn't possibly get all the work done that I would need to do just to meet deadlines. I was afraid, irrationally, that I would be disbarred for failing to meet the minimum standard for competent performance, which was to file documents on time. When anything turned out less than perfectly, I fretted. What could I have done better? What did I do wrong? Why did this judge seem to hate me? Why was the system so random, so mean-spirited, and so often stupid?

And I was angry. Angry that I worked such long days, yet had no money in the bank. Angry at how I gave to everyone in my life, yet reserved so little for myself. Angry that I was living in a small apartment that was cold and drafty in the winters and a sweatbox in the summers. If I took a break, I might not make payroll. Maybe it wouldn't happen the next week, but it would the next month.

That February, I also became preoccupied with the lawsuit against me. I often remained at home all day in my miserable apartment, sick and worried sick, going over and over each of the allegations against me, writing long, detailed e-mails and briefs, which I would send to my lawyers.

One day, Dane, a former law partner, reached me on my cell phone in my apartment. Dane and I had met when we were first-year associates at the same Wall Street law firm. Those Wall Street days were my first encounter with the pressures of my profession, and I had not handled them well. Dane often walked with me around Battery Park at lunch, making jokes and distracting me from my revenge fantasies featuring one of the firm's partners, who was making me miserable by forcing me through all-nighters, then asking questions like "Have you researched the law of England yet?"

Dane lives in Hawaii. He was in Los Angeles for some time off, and he thought he could cool me down by taking me for another walk. "Let's go hiking in the mountains," he said. "You can show me that old hotel you keep talking about." I was having none of it, of course. Instead of a relaxing trek up into the mountains, Dane got to be on the phone for an hour, running through issue after issue of the lawsuit against me. He told me to stop worrying. "I don't see how they can win that case," he said. He promised to read the briefs and give me his thoughts.

It was only because I was searching for a reason to write a thank-you note each day that I realized I should be more than just a little thankful for a friend like this. Years earlier,

I had left a partnership with Dane because I wanted to go out in pursuit of my "ideals." Although he had invested heavily in our partnership, his response was simple: "Life is very short. You need to do what you think will make you happy."

Now, burdened with his own cases, he gave up part of his vacation to listen to what any disinterested person would view as drivel, and then to give me advice worth hundreds of dollars an hour, for free. I could easily imagine what he must have felt like during this call. His head must have already been full of details of events, legal authorities, and deadlines of his own. "No, no more," his brain cells were calling out. "Not another legal problem!" Those were the words that invariably went through my mind whenever people called for free legal advice, which they often did. But during the thirty years of our friendship, Dane had listened countless times to long, meandering, whiny discourses from me, and he had always offered sympathy and solid professional advice, while enduring the obsessive thoughts that caused me to say the same thing over and over again.

How lucky was I to have a friend like this in my life? Why had it never occurred to me to write a simple note to thank him for his unselfish and unconditional friendship?

So I wrote him a note, observing that he had talked me off the wall again, just as he had nearly thirty years before:

Thank you for taking the time to read and consider the case against me, and to help me deal with my frustration. It seems that you are always the one who can calm me down when I start to lose perspective. As you did in 1979 when I almost took a swing at our favorite partner that one day on Wall Street.

In the worst moments of anger over how my life had turned out, I had failed to notice the treasure I had in such good friends. I had a friend—in fact, I had more than one—who would listen to me, who knew my overreactions for what they were, who could calm me down, who would keep me from letting my thoughts go down to a place from which I could not return.

During February, even while distressingly preoccupied with the lawsuit against me, I began to answer the question "How are you?" differently.

The time spent writing a couple thank-you notes at the end of the day cooled me down. It involved finding friends' or family members' addresses, which made me think about them and where they lived and what their life was like. In my spreadsheet, I typed out what I was thanking them for and a rough draft of the note itself. Then the actual writing of the note, in handwriting, also slowed me down. The handwriting took me back to my earlier days as a lawyer when my

work was all handwritten, in pencil, then taken to the ste-
nography pool at my first law firm, where Dane and I had
worked together. In those days the pencils were sharpened
by men in blue coats, who replaced them once a day. One of
them also took bets on sporting events.

Handwriting the notes also took me back to first grade,
when I'd labored over the Palmer method. My life as I sat
in those desks had still been relatively pure. By the time we
went to confession in the second grade, I had done only two
things of which I was ashamed. I still remember the kid I
hit just out of sight of the teachers and the stones I threw at
passing cars when I was four, just to see if I could hit one.
Now there was far more of which to be ashamed. I wished
for a life that carried only two sins. My handwriting, which
had degenerated into scribbling over the years, improved to
legibility as I made the drafting of the actual note an act like
prayer or meditation. I wanted the person receiving the note
to be able to read it.

After a half hour of writing thank-you notes, the murk
of my fear, upset, and self-pity seemed to dissipate, and I
often felt a little better.

One of the most comforting aspects of writing a thank-
you note was that it produced a tangible product. Although
I was giving it away and not keeping a copy, I felt I had in-
troduced something into the world that made a small positive difference. A piece of paper that would most certainly

have been thrown out had been turned into a concrete expression of gratitude to someone else—and would have a positive effect by reminding a person that they had touched me in a positive way. That seemed to give me a better sense of accomplishment than meditation or yoga.

During the time I worked on thank-you notes, I was focused on other people's lives instead of mine. As I gave more thought to whom I would be sending my next note, I realized how many people I had neglected to be grateful for. One of these, most surprisingly, was my apartment building manager, Mr. Robert.

Amid my frustration over the lawsuit against me, I could not sleep.

And though my insomnia was surely caused by my emotional disquiet, I often blamed external stresses—the heat, the noise, the light, the cold. In February, I blamed the toilet near my bedroom, which would not stop running. Night after night I lay awake listening to it turn on and off, needlessly wasting water, convinced that if it would only stop, then I could finally sleep.

I had been attracted to the hot-box apartment in Sierra Madre in part because the manager was a lithe young woman who seemed to fervently want me there. I did not consider Michelle a romantic possibility, except in fantasy, not only because she was far too young, but because she had a husband and three young children. Nevertheless, she was lovely and I looked forward to chatting with her about the smallest detail of my apartment's workings, the sink, the bathrooms, and so on.

In late 2007, however, this beautiful creature had been replaced by the curiously devoted Mr. Robert. Unlike Michelle, Mr. Robert dedicated himself to managing the building. Full time. He had carefully read the rules and regulations of the lease and the landlord's corporate gloss of said rules and regulations. I was annoyed by Mr. Robert's constant monitoring and intrusion in my life. Most of all I resented the corporation that thought he was an adequate replacement for Michelle.

I thought Mr. Robert an odd and rather spooky presence as he lumbered about. He seemed to always be looking at me sideways. He often knocked on my door out of the blue with his latest concern, which he needed to fully explain. Still, because of the running toilet, I needed his help. I had to stop avoiding him and actually approach him with my problem.

Mr. Robert seemed glad to act in his official capacity, and he responded that day with a squadron of plumbers. Of course, they could not find the problem. Nevertheless, as Mr. Robert stopped by to give an endless explanation, something he said inspired me with an answer that came to me in a flash of insight much like the insight Dr. Gregory House has in the fourth act of every episode of *House:* I could at least stop the noise by turning off the flow of water to the toilet.

At last, the toilet was quiet, and that night, and for a couple nights thereafter, until I could latch onto another external influence to blame, I slept well.

Using what I had been learning, I wrote a sincere note to Mr. Robert, thanking him for his quick reaction.

Dear Mr. Robert,

Thank you for responding so promptly to my concern. It always seems a little ridiculous when the concern is about the toilet, so thank you for taking it seriously. With the water turned way down, everything is fine, and it is sure a lot easier to sleep.

Best,
John (Apartment X)

The next week, a neatly printed note appeared on the wall of the apartment building, just above the mailboxes. Written in clear, even handwriting by Mr. Robert's wife, it explained that Mr. Robert had died. It turned out that he had been seriously ill from liver cancer and was waiting in vain for a liver transplant that never came. When he was trying to fix my toilet, he was in the last days of his life, watching the clock run out.

I decided to go to his funeral the next day at Rose Hills Memorial Park, a sort of down-market Forest Lawn on the smoggy east side of Los Angeles. This guy probably didn't have any friends, I thought, so maybe I should go so at least someone would be there to pay his respects. I was surprised to find that a crowd of more than a hundred of his friends had gathered to say good-bye. The ceremony ended with Mr. Robert's family releasing a bunch of white doves provided by Rose Hills. I found his widow, a quietly beautiful woman whom I had never noticed at the apartment. "A fabulous turnout," I said to her. "He had a lot of friends."

Mr. Robert's widow could sense that my understanding of Mr. Robert was limited to the apartment experience. "He was really a people person," she explained.

I had misjudged this dying man. At least I had not done so in the end, with the last words I said to him. Which were in my thank-you note.

After I wrote my note to Grace to thank her for her Christmas present, she e-mailed me: "Are you all right?" Yes, I replied, but next time we get together, I need to tell you something about thank-you notes.

She wondered whether that would be Friday. I said it would be Saturday. Our e-mails began to talk about how we missed being together. "I love to have your hand in mine, and my head on your shoulder," she wrote. And so we were back together.

We didn't discuss my New Year's resolution after that. But in addition to the e-mails and words with which we acknowledged the good things in our relationship, we started sending each other cards. "Your loving heart is so very comforting to me," she wrote shortly after Valentine's Day.

B y the end of February, when someone asked, "How are you?," instead of reporting the latest development in one of my struggles, I noted something for which I was grateful, even if it was only making payroll that week or keeping my business open. Often I mentioned that my youngest was doing well in school. She was always doing well in school, but it had just occurred to me to enjoy what a relief and a delight this success was to me.

The new way of responding to "How are you doing?" happened unconsciously, but after I noticed it, I decided it was something I should keep doing. From now on, the way I would answer this question would be by noting something for which I was grateful. I found myself using words like *thankful*, even *blessed*, though I was not a great believer in God or a very good churchgoer.

These early gains gave me some conviction that if I just

did this thank-you note project for a year, something would happen. In daring to hope, I was listening not only to my memories of my grandfather, but to very live advice from my father. My father has scoured American self-help litera-ture since his youth and was one of the first in his genera-tion to take a course from Dale Carnegie. Nevertheless, it was from one of his patients that he learned to always an-swer the "How are you?" question with the sentence "I'm on top of the world." After a month of thank-you notes, I ac-tually started to think of this as a realistic strategy, a way of uplifting the people around me.

For me, however, to be on top of the world, especially given the financial pressures I was under and the apartment in which I was living, was too flip an answer. But I was able to answer with something simple, good, and real, often what-ever I had written about in the previous night's thank-you note, and answering this way seemed to make me feel better about my life.

I began hoping I would not just *answer* differently about how I was doing, but that things would actually *be* different. I was finding I did have things for which I should be grate-ful. I soon realized that a year of gratitude could begin with the person I heard myself mentioning most often when people asked me how things were going. My daughter.

CHAPTER 6

Reading *Pollyanna* in Sierra Madre; or, Life as a Series of Fortunate Events

My seven-year-old daughter was with me three nights a week. We crowded together in the apartment with the darkening brown carpet that was a constant reminder to me of how low I had sunk. But my daughter viewed the place differently. She would regularly tell me that she thought it was the "best" apartment.

I had bought a cheap couch on sale at Wickes' Furniture—one of their many bankruptcy sales. The couch was made of a substance that was apparently invented to resemble leather, but it was colored a reddish hue not found on the hide of any healthy animal. In a small empty space behind this couch, my daughter established a realm she called her "fort." In it, she placed her books (*Nancy Drew, Harry Potter, High School Musical*, and so on), and her movies (movies about dogs, usually dogs that talked, like *The Shaggy Dog*, old and new versions), her artwork, and her easel. She could spend hours happily singing to herself in her fort, reading and working on her art projects, planning and designing her own space.

In the fort, my daughter wrote out stories and made lists of games she taught her schoolmates in the schoolyard. I found the rules and course of play for these games written out as the beginnings of a tome called *Games and How to Play*, describing games such as Catch a Square, Dance Around the Fire, and Owl Flight. The fort guarded souvenirs from each of our trips together over the years, pictures from the beach at San Diego and from the mountains near Big Bear, all neatly arranged on a bookshelf that held her favorite books and movies.

The fort stored my daughter's markers, scissors, paper, and journals. She would use our disparate collection of bleach-damaged beach towels to wall off the area while she sang and wrote and drew. In January 2008, the fort became a workshop where my daughter created a signature collection of miniature paper dogs and cats, which she cut out and gave to her schoolmates. These tiny figures became collectors' items in her class. They had names like Annakin, Spot, Sunflower, Pumpkin, Maya, Zack, Peanuts, and Honey. The funny little names dictated the appearance of these animals. For example, Candy Cane had red and white stripes, Storm had blue and white swirls. Pumpkin was pumpkin-colored. The dog named L.A. had sunglasses. In her journal, she wrote adventures for these characters. My favorite was called "The Meow, Meow Club," which was also the name of the "in" place where all her creatures would meet.

We started reading books together when it was time for bed. We had talked a bit about Heath Ledger; his death had been one of those stories so pervasively covered in the media that even seven-year-olds could not avoid it. I explained that reading and listening to books were what we did to fall asleep. She agreed that it made much more sense to fall asleep our way. As she began falling asleep, I would lower the volume of my voice, and then stop reading altogether. After waiting silently for a few minutes, I would get up, but she would often startle and say, "No, don't stop." I would lean over and kiss her and assure her she was already asleep.

We were trying out some things that were advanced for her—or so I thought. She liked the Harry Potter series, and I appreciated the way the complicated magical conflicts of that magnum opus would quickly put her to sleep. We also tried Lemony Snicket's *Series of Unfortunate Events* books. I liked the way all difficult words in the Lemony Snicket

books were immediately explained so that I did not have to double as a human dictionary, a job at which I did not always excel. My daughter, however, did not seem to identify with the series of unfortunate events encountered by the Baudelaire orphans, and despite the magnetic attraction of the well-written prose, we stopped after two books.

In early 2008, my daughter left the Harry Potter volume we were reading at school, and we had to hunt in the dark and vacuum-neglected crevices of the apartment for something to read. On the floor behind the dresser, along with some hairpins, candy wrappers, and paper clips, we found a discarded paperback copy of a work that had long been in the public domain. A few years earlier, we had purchased a copy of Eleanor H. Porter's 1913 classic, *Pollyanna.* The book had been too advanced for my daughter when we first bought it; she had really been attracted only to the shiny locket with which the book was packaged. Yet given there was nothing else to read in February 2008, in our cheap apartment in Sierra Madre, my daughter and I started reading *Pollyanna*, which was set in 1913 Vermont.

I could only read my daughter to sleep on Wednesday, Thursday, and Friday nights—I was left with my longing for her company on the other four nights. *Pollyanna* has thirty-two chapters. At a chapter a night, which was our usual pace, it would have taken quite a while for us to get through the book. But her interest was captured from the start. This

surprised me. The book has little action. Even the car accident that befalls Pollyanna at the end is barely described. And the dialogue is so filled with turn-of-the-last-century slang, even I had trouble following it. My daughter took it in raptly, though, and begged me for three chapters at a time, then four.

I had thought of Pollyanna in the way the word is used in the vernacular, as a naïve and absurdly wishful person. When I read the book, however, I realized that Pollyanna was not in the least naïve; rather, she was able to recognize the value of being faithful to gratitude. She liked to play what she called the "glad game." In every situation, no matter how dire, she liked to find something to feel glad about. While this sounds a bit silly, it was actually a courageous reaction to the enormous tragedy she confronted at age eleven.

The "glad game" was Pollyanna's only significant inheritance from her father, an idealistic young missionary who took his young family to the West, where he and his young wife both died, in a shabby town, far from the young woman's wealthy, disapproving family in Vermont. Pollyanna's dying father had taught her the "glad game" in hopes that it would help her deal with the poverty and loneliness he knew would follow his death. The game started one day when Pollyanna inexplicably received crutches instead of the doll for which she had begged her parents. She explained the game to Nancy, her aunt's servant:

Pollyanna laughed again, but she sighed, too; and in the gathering twilight her face looked thin and wistful.

"Why, we began it on some crutches that came in a missionary barrel."

"CRUTCHES!"

"Yes. You see I'd wanted a doll, and father had written them so; but when the barrel came the lady wrote that there hadn't any dolls come in, but the little crutches had. So she sent 'em along as they might come in handy for some child, sometime. And that's when we began it. . . . The game was to just find something about everything to be glad about—no matter what 'twas," rejoined Pollyanna, earnestly. "And we began right then—on the crutches."

"Well, goodness me! I can't see anythin' ter be glad about—gettin' a pair of crutches when you wanted a doll!"

Pollyanna clapped her hands.

"There is—there is," she crowed. "But I couldn't see it, either, Nancy, at first," she added, with quick honesty. "Father had to tell it to me."

"Well, then, suppose YOU tell ME," almost snapped Nancy.

"Goosey! Why, just be glad because you don't— NEED—'EM!" exulted Pollyanna, triumphantly.

As everyone who has seen the movie knows, Pollyanna will eventually need the crutches, and then even the glad game cannot save her. Only the love she has earned by teaching the glad game to others saves her from the despair that she suffers when she is told she can no longer walk.

At the beginning, however, the glad game is all that the young orphan has to help her deal with the tragedy of the loss of her parents. Contrary to our modern view of Pollyanna, she is not a lobotomized ninny who doesn't notice the true nature of her plight. Her sorrow about the death of her parents is always just below the surface of her outward struggle to be glad.

Neither is Pollyanna naïve, or ignorant of the tragedy of her life. She knows that she is poor, that other people do not live out of a barrel or at the mercy of the Ladies' Aid. The glad game is just a device to give her the courage to rise above her tragedy, and eventually it puts to shame the self-obsessed adults in the town who believe they are struggling, though the lives they perceive as horrible in fact contain more than a fair share of blessings.

Pollyanna senses the cold hearts of the adults around her. She is well aware that her aunt Polly is cruel and self-centered. When Aunt Polly decides Pollyanna must live in a hot, stuffy attic, despite the many vacant, more comfortable bedrooms on the lower floors, the insult is not lost on

Pollyanna, and even she cannot find anything to be glad about, as she tells her dead father while sobbing into her sheets: "I know, father-among-the-angels, I'm not playing the game one bit now—not one bit; but I don't believe even you could find anything to be glad about sleeping all alone way off up here in the dark—like this."

As we read Pollyanna's story in our own stuffy "attic," my daughter noticed Aunt Polly's coldness. She asked me to explain Aunt Polly's actions, and I explained that she acted out of duty rather than love. We talked about how different it would be if when we saw each other we hugged out of duty instead of out of love. We had fun acting out dutiful hugs until we laughed. I started explaining that Aunt Polly did not know how to love. With a television-watching child's sense of the happy ending, my daughter predicted that Pollyanna was going to teach her how.

We read that Pollyanna, trying to avoid suffocation in her stuffy attic, opened a window, letting in a few flies. Aunt Polly threw a tantrum and punished Pollyanna by forcing her to read a tract on the dangerous germs carried by flies. My daughter laughed, calling Aunty Polly a "drama queen." In one of the many moments when there is sarcasm as well as wonder in Pollyanna's voice, she tells her aunt that she "never saw anything so perfectly lovely and interesting" in her life as the tract on the dangers of flies. Like all of those who have misjudged Pollyanna since, Aunt Polly cannot hear the sarcasm and dismisses her wise and witty niece as a peculiar and frustrating child.

Porter's book has a quaint phraseology that was also fun for us. In *Pollyanna*, people don't inhale, they "draw in breaths." The first time my daughter noticed this phrase was when "Nancy drew in a breath." We had been reading some Nancy Drew mysteries, so my daughter wondered how Nancy Drew had gotten into the story. After much explanation, and a coughing fit resulting from my attempts at demonstrating the drawing in of breath, my daughter and I took turns giving the long speech that caused Nancy to draw in a breath in the first place. We were gasping and laughing. Then I had to explain how Pollyanna drew a breath in "tremulously," as if she were about to cry, and we went through that too. In *Pollyanna*, people don't shout when excited; instead they "ejaculate" their words. I decided I would just change this word and breeze over it, rather than try to explain the meaning that Eleanor Porter intended in this instance, only to have my daughter unwittingly introduce the word in her second-grade classroom.

After we had finished the book, we started C. S. Lewis's *The Magician's Nephew*. But a few nights into it, she said, "Dad, can you read me *Pollyanna*?"

"But we just finished it."

"I want to read it again."

This had not happened since *Go, Dog. Go!* and other simple books I'd read to her when she was two or three. Something about this story had touched her. The second time through was even more fun.

For me, the small oppressive apartment in Sierra Madre seemed much like Aunt Polly's airless attic. Living there was made worse by my self-imposed exile from the house I had paid for, and was still paying for, but no longer lived in. Yet my daughter, while fully aware that her cousins and schoolmates lived in much nicer places, cared not at all. She viewed our apartment as a place where we could spend time together, and that, to her, was enough. As I came to understand her perspective, I tried to look at our situation the same way.

In February, my daughter persuaded me to get past my historical indifference to animals and to adopt a cat, Brody. We found Brody in a pet product chain store, where a local woman who rescued cats had set up a row of cages with homeless kittens for people to consider for adoption. "He seemed to really want to be with me," my daughter would explain later when asked why it was this cat she chose, after holding several in her arms.

I wrote a note to the woman who had cared for Brody before placing him with us:

Thank you for fostering Brody, and then working with us on the adoption. He is a delightful cat, extremely playful, loving, and affectionate. We are hoping to give him a good home that will confirm for you the effectiveness of your altruistic efforts to save him.

By this time in late February, I had written more than fifty thank-you notes. I was way past the weirdness of writing a thank-you note to a cat lady.

Brody's long hair had disgusting clumps he couldn't quite clean, but he was soon ours, well groomed and so aggressive he jumped off the second-floor balcony of our apartment to check out the rest of the world one morning. We chased after him together in our pajamas and brought him back to our attic, where my daughter enclosed him with her in her fort.

Brody belonged to my daughter, but he kept me company when I was alone and missing her.

The apartment complex had a small pool, none too clean and completely unheated, but my daughter insisted we try it. So one winter evening, she dove right in and screamed with laughter at the freezing water. I told her it might be a good idea for me to watch. "Be a man!" she challenged. After that, I jumped in.

Over the next year, we planted hibiscus, and morning

glories that hung from our balcony. We grew our own basil, which became part of the special pasta we made on Wednesday nights. The walls of the little apartment filled with my daughter's artwork.

The owners started to improve the building, and eventually two teachers from my daughter's school moved in, which bestowed special status on her among her mates at school. "My apartment is famous," she proclaimed.

My daughter and *Pollyanna* broke through my morose obsession with my own little stuffy attic. And with the help of my thank-you note project, my own glad game, I began to realize that very few of the people I knew who lived in better houses, or had more money, had a relationship like the one I had with my daughter.

I worried that our happiness in each other might not last, but this was an example of how I had always viewed my own life as a series of unfortunate events—despite living parents and a fairly comfortable middle-class upbringing.

Yet there was something powerful in my daughter's internal makeup that led her to view her life as a series of fortunate events. You could ask her, and she would list the good things that happened to her on a given day. If you forced her to turn off the television, she would be grumpy for a few moments, but soon would be embedded in an art project or a game design in her fort.

One day, I could think of nothing in my world for which

to be thankful. The anguish of the past year threatened to retake me. I could think of no one to whom I wanted to write a thank-you note. I had been struggling for days with the lawsuit against me, while trying to keep up with my work. That day, instead of writing a thank-you note, I sent a lengthy letter to my lawyers, refuting every argument and accusation against me in elegantly turned phrases. I knew from previous experience in this case that my lawyers would only pretend to read this material. I pictured the meeting in their offices where they dismissed my memos, saying, "He's way too close to this." I had said that myself many times after reviewing similarly tortured writings from my clients.

Two days later, I lost my tenuous cool and lipped off at the young lawyer who was delegated to ask me if I wanted anything else in the statement they gave me to sign. Nothing, I replied, other than the pages of material I had labored over. When she said she had written the brief I had asked the partners to write, I demanded to speak to them. In the ensuing conversation, their efforts at patiently justifying their minimalist approach seemed increasingly affected. Finally, frustrated by my resistance, one of them started to solemnly intone the adage, often attributed to Abraham Lincoln, that he who has himself for a lawyer has a fool for a client, in a tone that suggested this might be a new idea for me, and perhaps I should give some thought to it.

I knew exactly what my lawyers were thinking, because

I'd had those same thoughts so many times before. Yet I was different, I told myself. Unlike the views of the many clients I had felt were too close to their cases, my views should have been treated with seriousness, because I was a member of that tiny club of people who really knew what they were doing.

In my view, my lawyers were too proud to accept my comments. I was frustrated and depressed, thinking that I was probably going to lose a case that should have been won, and it was going to cost me not just money but my reputation, and potentially a career.

But then I picked up my daughter, and as almost always she was cheerful. She had had a great day at school because she had her favorite class (her favorite seemed to change almost every day), and her favorite after-school program, Animal Invasion, where she got to meet and pet unusual animals. She practiced her piano and we had pizza. I read her *Pollyanna*. We talked that night about the things that she didn't have that she wanted, and she listed off a few that seemed like they might not be happening on my present budget, including a flat-screen television. So I asked her about the things she did have that she wanted, and her face lit up. She talked about her cats and her dog and her stuffed animals.

That night I wrote a thank-you note to her and left it on her bed, where she had fallen asleep while I was reading.

I knew for sure that my note had been about the one thing in life for which I should be most thankful. In the morning, I had to read the note to her because she didn't yet read cursive very well.

> *My daughter,*
>
> *Thank you for being cheerful and happy when I pick you up in the evening. Sometimes I don't have a very fun day, but when I see you and we talk about things, and have fun, I feel better. Thank you for being the best daughter ever.*
>
>

Love,
Dad

She kept this note behind the drapes of the window by her bed, with some special rocks and coins.

I will never forget the night I wrote that thank-you note and left it with my sleeping daughter. For me, it represented a turning point, away from the low where I had found myself in December 2007. I had identified something in my life that made me richer than all of the people I envied.

My life would continue to be vexing and difficult for much of the coming year. But I would never again question whether it was worth living. I started paying attention whenever I crossed the street, even when the WALK sign was on, because I knew there were drivers who wouldn't see the light. No matter what else happened to me, there was something I didn't want to miss.

CHAPTER 7

An End of Winter

I sat in a courtroom behind my lawyers, waiting for the hearing on the lawsuit against me. My fears cycled through my mind. The chairs were thirty years old, wooden, and bolted together. The backs were shaped in a curve that no human back could possibly rest against comfortably, but that was the least of my discomfort.

My lawyers had not asked me to go up to the counsel table with them, feeling, no doubt, that I had nothing positive to contribute. Actually, they probably had not even wanted me at the hearing.

In announcing his appearance for the

record, the opposing lawyer noted that his name began with *W,* and that this also stood for *Winner.* The judge seemed taken with some of this lawyer's "winning" arguments and decided to take the briefs back to his chambers and rule at a later date.

The next day, however, the judge ruled that the case did not justify further proceedings. He dismissed it and ordered the other side to pay for my attorneys. There would be an appeal, but for now, the veil was lifting a bit.

I wrote a thank-you note to my lawyer:

Thank you for your hard work and expertise. Your victory will help me focus on my personal and professional life. For today, W *stands only for your win.*

I sent it with a bottle of champagne.

Winter was over with a *W.* Much of my fear and anguish had lifted. Maybe something bigger than I'd originally imagined was coming out of this thank-you note thing, I thought, though I wasn't yet sure what this bigger change might be.

CHAPTER 8

Thank You for Paying Your Bills

Our offices had been uncomfortably crowded for a while, but in March they became unbearable, at least to me. Two part-time lawyers shared an office. A third worked in a hallway outside my office, because we had no real office for him. Now that we were planning to move, things became even worse. Files packed in boxes cluttered offices and hallways. The pictures of family and mementos of the past, the little things that made our workplace a home, were packed away.

Although we knew we needed to move, we had no place to go. Our situation grew tense. Our landlord issued vague, then explicit, legal threats. In one he noted it was time to "act immediately" and to "take legal action," then he termed my offer to pay rent at a higher rate during this unplanned holdover period "a Band-Aid for a lost limb."

Like our impatient landlord, we felt the need to "act immediately," and had signed a letter of intent to move into the first available space that could accommodate us. The floor plan, which featured a large empty space in the middle, did not match our needs, but at least there was plenty of room; we figured we would adapt. We did not have time to wait around for the perfect space. Even when we agreed to terms, however, it took weeks to get the new landlord to review and sign the lease.

Meanwhile, amid the growing clutter in our "waiting area" (it was too small to be a "waiting room"), our existing landlord's representative would sit for extended periods of time, waiting to get the latest news about our move. I often did not see this, because I was using a bout with the spring flu as an excuse to work from the lair of my uncomfortable apartment—avoiding the overcrowding of the office and seeking privacy from which to figure out my next desperate move. While our old landlord pondered what damage he would assess for our holdover, our new landlord mulled over asking for more money up front, and I considered liquidating my retirement account in order to make the deposit on the new space, which would be $23,450.

Sitting on the dirty linen of a $35 Ikea chair in my apartment, I worried that my employees, who had not received their Christmas bonuses for the first time in my firm's history, would become as rattled by these events as I was. I decided to write a thank-you note to each of the employees who had not received a Christmas bonus, thanking them for what they continued to do so well. The first of these was to my paralegal, Larina, a wonder who worked feverishly and passionately from the moment she arrived in the morning till the moment she left in the early evening. She answered the phones, kept the files up to date and in perfect order, filed the documents with the court, and acted as a secretary to all of the lawyers, sending out and filing the crushing daily volume of pleadings and correspondence. About five times a day, I would call out to Larina, and she would come running, then go and find some obscure file or document that I would randomly believe was the most important thing to consider at that particular moment. She also made the coffee and washed the coffee cups.

I was just reflecting in amazement at how remarkable it is that you are able to keep everything in order in our office. Nothing could be accomplished here—at all—without your work. Thank you for everything you do each day to keep our firm in motion.

In March, as the date we were supposed to leave came and went, the tension surrounding our move ratcheted up further. But no one quit. Instead, the lawyers and staff continued to do their work as efficiently as before, just stepping around the boxes and the landlord's lurking representative. They remained cheerful and upbeat. My wonderful paralegal wrote back to me:

> *I received your card and in response to that, I say you are always welcome. The motivation and drive I have to work so hard is because of who you are and how you treat people with respect, care, and consideration. It is nice to know that my work is important and being appreciated. I wish and pray to GOD that His blessings and His guidance and protection are with us always. John, 2008 will be a great year.*

Then, as lovely as her note was, an even more unexpected thing happened. In my e-mail in-box, I began to read sentiments of gratitude and praise being sent among all of my firm's employees and attorneys. They were thanking one another and sending me a copy or, sometimes, writing to me directly to tell me what a fantastic job one of their colleagues was doing. One related how Larina had "prepared an almost 1,000-page document production in probably less than one full work day that included extensive redactions, Bates labeling and the rest. Of course she did this with her customary good cheer and dedication." Another noted of her coworker that "she is a very valuable and loyal employee and good friend to all of us. I know she's been especially happy the last few days because she's had so much work." Another said, "We should not take her for granted."

The notes written by my employees about their coworkers were the beginnings of the reactions to my thank-you notes that would eventually surround my life, and would keep me writing more thank-you notes.

Around this time, Bob asked me to lunch. After our breakfast on December 22, 2007, he must have braced himself whenever he called, wondering how long he could make good on his promise to check up on a self-centered depressive whose life was going down the tubes. Yet by March, whenever he called, he heard cheery news about my daughter's latest accomplishment and praise for the others in my firm. Even before the case against me was dismissed, he had noticed that something was different about me; he was more than a little mystified.

When he called about lunch, I chose Pie 'n Burger, a traditional diner at the base of Pasadena's business district.

I had a Chili Size, which, at Pie 'n Burger, is a fresh hamburger patty smothered in a long plate of mild, canned chili, covered with fresh onions and served with a hamburger bun just toasted on the grill. Everything at Pie 'n Burger is decidedly ordinary, but it's freshly served. You sit only two steps away from the counter, and the food is picked up promptly from the grill and placed in front of you in one continuous sweep of the server's hand. The time from grill to customer can be as short as fifteen seconds. The coffee is Apffels, an institutional brand, but it is always absolutely fresh, brewed in clean coffee pots; it just seems like pure caffeine pleasure. I like having people bring me coffee in the morning, and the people at Pie 'n Burger, especially Kathleen, bring it with a sincere sweetness.

After Bob and I had moved on from our burgers to the impossibly tall lemon meringue pie, he told me that he had seen a complete change in my demeanor from the previous December.

"Some things you are describing to me are better, but some are worse. Yet you seem changed. You sounded better on the phone, and you look so much better. What's up with you?"

And so Bob became a confidant of my thank-you note project. His eyes widened as I ran through some of my early results—the loan repayments from my sons, the notes my coworkers were sending one another. And now I told him about the most wondrous development of all: my clients were paying their bills.

I had long resisted the obvious way to collect bills: pressuring nonpaying clients to pay or leave. Collecting on bills was the last thing I ever wanted to do for a job. The part of the law I like is the intellectual challenge—figuring out what the law is, then writing a persuasive argument bringing that law to bear on the facts. Bill collecting was never at all fun for me, even in the best of times. And the truth is a lot of people don't pay their lawyers. Sometimes this is because they see no value in the service after it is delivered. This view is often not irrational. In many cases even the best lawyering does no good for the client; in fact, it may only make their problems worse. At times, I felt embarrassed to be part of what many view as societal cancer. When I admitted to being a lawyer at a party, I often added: "Don't hold it against me."

Bob had long advised me to get tough, or at least to narrow the practice to the clients who paid. "You have plenty of clients who will pay your bills," he said. "Why not just work for them?"

I now explained to Bob how my thank-you note project had given me the idea for a different approach. In January and February, I took a look at the checks that did come in and decided to thank those clients who were paying, especially the ones who were paying on time.

One client was located just down the street but had operations all over the country. My bills were paid out of two far-off places, yet the payments were nearly always made on time. I noticed a couple payments that were especially early:

> *Many thanks to you for seeing that our bills are paid on time. We received payment today from Van Wert, Ohio, and Kalamazoo, Michigan, on bills that were barely two weeks old. This keeps our business functioning smoothly, frees me from worry, and is just all around terrific.*

As people often did throughout that year, this client called me to thank me for my thank-you note. He told me how he spent a lot of time processing large payments for law firms, yet the only time he ever heard from partners was to complain about the fact that payments were late. Often the complaints went to his superior. Later, visiting him, I found my thank-you note pinned up on his bulletin board. For a while all of our bills to this client were paid in two weeks.

I was learning to cherish such clients, many of whom were envied by other law firms. And because I was paying closer attention to which clients were paying on time, if only so I could write one of my 365 notes, I began to notice which clients were falling behind on their bills and to intervene and stop problems before they grew so big they could destroy my profit for the year.

B ut over pie at Pie 'n Burger, Bob and I did not just talk about me and how my bills were getting paid. My younger son had recently had a setback at his job, and I was worried about him. In helping me through these worries, Bob shared similar struggles he was going through with his daughter. He had brought these up before, at that frightful, depressing December 22 breakfast, but I hadn't really heard him then. Now I was listening. I realized that Bob had struggles too. Both of us had tears in our eyes as we talked these problems through.

At the end of the lunch, Bob said, "You know, I was worried about you in December, but I think you're going to make it just fine." He again picked up the tab for lunch. So I wrote him a thank-you note:

Thank you so much for taking me to one of my favorite places for lunch. It felt like my birthday. Thanks for all the time you've spent talking through my recent issues, and being there for me in my moments of crisis. Thank you too for having the courage to share with me the difficulties that you have had—it reminds me that others face greater challenges

and are able to summon far greater courage than is asked of
me. I was moved by your confidence that I would make it.
By listening, and caring, you have made a tremendous
difference in my life.

Even now, I am a bit embarrassed by how open I was be-coming about my feelings that spring. I come from a generation in which men are taught not to say such things.

Now that Bob knew about my thank-you note project, I would occasionally send him updates. For example, I for-warded him the hopeful e-mails going around my office. As he received these throughout the year, he began calling them "the anthology of gratitude." Getting these e-mails must have been a welcome change from the tales of woe Bob had previ-ously endured whenever he asked me how it was going.

I also come from a generation in which it is typical to fight for the tab at the end of a meal with friends. Of course, there are those occasions in which the other person never puts up a fight, but those are not the friends you care that much about, or perhaps they aren't friends at all.

During my thank-you year, I did not fight for the tab. This started with Bob picking it up on December 22 and my son picking it up when he repaid the loan. In other words, it started because I flat out couldn't afford to pick up the tab. But as the year went on and my finances stabilized, I quietly reminded myself that in being someone's guest for a meal I had one more thing to be thankful for. Not always being the one to pay the check was now an accomplishment of sorts, because I would write one more of my 365 notes. The thank-you notes I sent to friends who bought me lunch was a reminder that I had generous friends. I would say how much I appreciated their friendship and their generosity. The thank-you note for each meal served as a marker and reminder to me that the next time it was my turn to reach for the check. Sometimes I pay, sometimes someone else does, but fights over restaurant bills are no longer part of my life.

Seeing how many of these thank-you notes I'd written at the end of the year, I was surprised at just how often someone was buying me lunch.

CHAPTER 9

Thank the Starbucks Guy

By the end of January, I had written forty-three thank-you notes, more than one a day, but by March I had begun to let the writing of notes ebb and flow with my emotions. I used my spreadsheet to note the people and things for which I was grateful, then I would write five or ten notes at a time. Each of those sessions felt as calming as yoga.

Even ninety days into the project, however, despite all of the encouraging things that were happening, my life was still deeply flawed. At any moment, the web of troubles that had brought me to despair in December could reinvigorate itself and make me miserable again. Even an overheard remark could bring it back, because all thoughts, of whatever kind, reminded me how much of a loser I had felt at that moment. In March, this happened when I was reminded of the unobtainability of a career dream.

In the summer of 2006, I began the long application process to be a judge. I had been waiting for the right moment to fill out this application ever since I had become a lawyer twenty-seven years earlier. Almost from the moment I understood the adversarial legal system, I wanted to make myself qualified to be a judge. I longed to work only to find the truly right result, at least the right result required by the law, instead of just the result the client had hired me to obtain. I had kept this goal in mind throughout my legal career, and in 2006 I finally felt my qualifications were sufficient, and I was ready for the next step.

On the application, I had responded with candor about my career as well as about private aspects of my life. By the time of the first interview with the nominating committee, in early 2007, I had forgotten about the candid answers, and I went to the interview expecting to talk only of my qualifications and my hopes for the job. After a few minutes surveying my qualifications, however, the interviewing panel focused on my weaknesses: my lack of experience in criminal law and my disclosures regarding my personal life. I believed that the matters I had disclosed had no real effect upon my performance as a lawyer; they had never impacted my cases or clients. Yet I left the interview feeling that these disclosures were the main concern of the interviewers and that because of them my application had no chance of succeeding.

I was not called to a second interview. By mid-2007, all of the judicial vacancies in Los Angeles County were filled. By the time I reached the nadir of December 2007, I had mentally added my failed judicial application to the flaming pyre of losses from that year.

This wound was partly healing in the glow of my first ninety thank-you notes in early 2008 when someone reviewing the applications was quoted in the legal press saying, "I have information about people that the general public doesn't have. I can never say why a person who in public seems wonderful, kind, and personable I can't consider."

I focused on this official's use of the word *kind.* I knew that some of my references had used that word to describe me. Was she talking about me? Almost certainly not. Yet this was how personally I could take a casual comment at the time, as if the only drama going on in the world was my own.

Playing Pollyanna's glad game, I tried to find a way to be happy *because* I would not attain this career goal. After all, I could be glad that I had managed to be kind to a few people in the course of a decades-long legal career. And I could be glad that I had not compromised my personal integrity with a clever response to questions about my personal life.

Still, the night after I read this official's comment, even though the water in the toilet was no longer running, I was unable to sleep. In fact, I was often sleepless that March. Sometimes the only way I could nod off during this period was to watch multiple episodes of *The X Files* or *The Sopranos.* I found something soothing in the never-ending debate between Scully and Mulder: Were the aliens to blame for the boy's death in this episode or was the death perfectly explainable by modern forensic science? Well, let's open up the body and see. When watching *The X Files* didn't work, I would turn to *The Sopranos,* looking into a clean, middle-class neighborhood to see yet another lovably evil character whacked with extreme prejudice. That these stories calmed me should perhaps have been disquieting. But on the night after the legal press had reminded me of my lost chance for a judicial appointment, my ongoing worries kept even these shows from relaxing me into sleep. When the morning alarm went off, I lay as awake as I'd been all night, thinking it would be easier not to get up.

I had not written a thank-you note the previous day. Mired in self-pity, I could think of no one to thank.

Finally, I got up.

On my way to the office, I stopped at Starbucks. There was a guy at this Starbucks who was especially cheery, sometimes jarringly so to someone not yet caffeinated. Not only was he vibrating with enthusiasm, but he had taken the time to learn some of the customers' names, including mine. Maybe there is an employee manual in which they are told to do this, but this guy struck me as sincere. On this morning, he greeted me with "Good morning, John, the usual venti?" When he first remembered my name, I had tried to remember his, but I got it wrong and called him Steve for a while. Then there was a period when I didn't try because I was never sure: Was it Scott or was it Steve? Suddenly, I realized that I had something to be thankful for. I had my thank-you note for this day. Now all I needed was a name. So I lingered at a table with my coffee for a while until another customer, with a better memory, said, "Thanks, Scott."

So, as absurd as it may seem, I wrote a thank-you note to the Starbucks guy:

Scott,

Thank you for taking the time each morning to greet me in a friendly way. It is also so wonderful to me that you took the time and trouble to remember my name. In this day

and age, few people make this effort, and fewer still do it in a
way that feels sincere. You do both. It really makes a
difference to me every day.

Best,

I handed him the note the next morning, after he gave me my venti, and his cheery eyes fell a shade. He put it aside. I wondered why he did not smile. When I went in the following day, Scott explained. He had recently been put in a management position, he said, and his day was largely spent on customer complaints. Something about paying three dollars for a cup of coffee makes people feel they can spend endless amounts of other people's time making sure that their "experience" is absolutely perfect, and that they should voice their opinion about every aspect of the experience. So when I gave him the note, he was wearily thinking it was yet another customer complaint, and from someone who had seemed like a nice customer, no less. Scott had been taken aback to discover my envelope had only a simple statement of gratitude.

As strained as it may seem to be writing a thank-you note to the guy at Starbucks, my appreciation was genuine. Corporate homogenization has taken the personal aspect out of most of our commercial interactions. Much of our work has been replaced by machines, and when it is not, we take out our frustration on those who do the remaining human

work, expecting them to function like machines and for-
getting these are often the same low-paid individuals who
may be the next to lose their jobs. To me, it seemed that Scott
and I had forged a tiny bit of human warmth in this erod-
ing wasteland.

And he taught me a lesson—that there is value in the
smallest note, and in being thankful for what seems like the
smallest thing. This interaction reawakened my sense that
unpredictable good would happen if I wrote 365 thank-you
notes and that I needed to follow through.

During this period of my life, I didn't get many social
invitations. Focused on my daughter and absorbed by
the survival of my little firm, I had grown isolated from the
friends I had made at the big firm and the big corporation
where I had previously worked. But Ron, my old corporate
boss, who had a beautiful home in South Pasadena, had not
forgotten me, and in late winter he had invited my daughter and me to dinner. I was lucky enough to sit next to another of Ron's friends, Steve, a lawyer from Billings, Montana,
with whom I had worked a decade before on a lengthy trial
in Montana.

Steve had been chosen as the lead lawyer on our team then
because of his ability to communicate well with the judge.
What I remembered while sitting with him that evening out

in South Pasadena was not just his ability, but how he expressed hard, uncomfortable truth with genuine kindness. So many lawyers are spoiled by their talents and brains into becoming somewhat evil geniuses. Rewarded for verbally destroying the ideas of others, they are drawn to the assumption that others desire them to repeat this behavior as often as possible.

In court, Steve's strength was the simple way he said everything, and that everything he said was the truth. Outside the courtroom, his gentle nature was a joy. He did not look down on you in the way that most outside counsel look down on in-house counsel; he just enjoyed your presence, whoever you were. He made you feel like you were good company. Steve kept a bottle of Bombay in the freezer and was always available for sequences of martinis.

While I sat with Steve at the dinner party in early 2008, he recalled that he had recommended me for the judicial position I had applied for in 2006. I was touched. From my unsuccessful bid to become a judge I had taken away only bitterness, but Steve reminded me that there was much in the experience for which I should be grateful. More than fifty men and women had filled out forms recommending me for the position. Some, like Steve, were far better lawyers than I could ever hope to be. So, after reconnecting at dinner, I wrote Steve a thank-you note:

It was so good to see you and your wife the other night. It made me wish that I had stayed in my old corporate job so we could have worked together more. Thank you for taking the time to respond to the inquiries regarding my nomination. It felt good to know you would recommend me. Wish we could have had a few more martinis together too.

The next spring, as my thank-you project came to a close, Steve died playing golf on a Montana golf course.

My thank-you note had been the last thing I said to him. It was also the first time I had shown gratitude for something that occurred in my quest to be a judge.

A few weeks later, a new panel of attorneys called to interview me for the judicial position again. This time the interview went well, and the disclosures that had given me trouble in my previous interview seemed to be perceived in perspective with the rest of my career. Leaving the interview, I withdrew my focus from myself for a minute and thought about the attorneys who had conducted the interview. This process was purely a volunteer affair for them. Both were busy, distinguished attorneys who had taken hours away from their jobs just for my interview. And when it was over, they would write a report about it. The interview might end up being a meaningless exercise for me, but it was certain from the start that these hours of uncompensated effort would never result in any gain for these two people.

So I wrote thank-you notes to each of them:

Thank you for taking the time out of your schedule to interview me and to work with the Evaluation Committee reviewing my application. The work you do is valuable to the community, yet anonymous and unsung. I appreciated the atmosphere that put me at ease for the discussion of matters both personal and professional, handling them thoroughly, but with tact.

The dinner at which I saw my friend Steve also reminded me of my debt to Ron, my old corporate boss, who had invited my daughter and me to his house that night.

In 1997, 1998, and 1999, I had been working at a major corporation when Ron put me in for some stock options. Ron was a good boss, but also a brilliant attorney. So for the most part, when he distributed options, he was just sharing the credit for his own good ideas with those who were willing to work hard with him to implement his strategies.

As the stock market rose with home prices after 2003, the options I had received in the previous decade became more valuable each year. I began to think of these options as the foundation for my ultimate retirement dream, buying a sailboat and sailing the world with anyone who wanted to come along.

In 2007, I had to sell the options to meet my living expenses and to make payroll. The dream was gone, I thought.

At dinner that night at Ron's house, I focused for the first time not on the loss of the options, but on the fact that I had them in the first place. Had I not had them, I would no longer have a job and neither would anyone else working with me. My business had survived a year of zero profit with no financial margin to spare, but without those options, it would not have survived at all.

So a couple days after this dinner, I wrote to my old boss to acknowledge how the options had saved me:

They're all gone now, and I need to tell you now how grateful I am for the stock options you gave me a decade ago. Last year was a difficult year because of so many clients not paying, and other difficulties best left undescribed. In short, my operation would not have survived without these options, yet it has survived, and seems to be headed in the right direction. It reminded me of how important your guidance and friendship have been to my career. Thank you.

I had been bitter about the need to sell those options just to buy groceries and pay utilities. I hated letting go of my sailboat dream. But now I felt how lucky I was to have had the margin in which to commit errors. As we all know now, the stock market crashed in 2008 and reached bottom in early 2009, just at the time I had planned to sell the options right before their expiration. Had I kept them, they would have been worthless. To any dream.

As my focus moved from the painful reversals of 2007 to the resources and friends that had helped me survive them, I started to feel that things were getting better. But then I'd wonder, Were things really getting better or was this hopeful feeling just a trick of my mind?

On March 5, 2008, the financial press reported rumors that Bear Stearns, one of the nation's oldest investment banks, was in financial trouble. It was the first of the truly surreal financial news reports that became commonplace during 2008. By March 13, 2008, Bear Stearns had collapsed and would be no more, taken over by its rival, J.P. Morgan. This development was incredible to me. From my work on mortgage fraud cases, I had seen, close up, the excesses of the mortgage market. Yet I believed that so many politicians, both Democrat and Republican, had pushed and primed the existence of this market so much that the government could never let it collapse. This market had replaced the tech boom of the nineties and become the driving force of the economy. It could not be allowed to fail. Yet, now the virus of bad mortgages infected the world financial markets with the force of a plague, and venerable institutions were evaporating. Maybe failure could not be prevented.

Most of my clients were in the mortgage business, and many had begun to suffer. One of these, a mortgage company based in Georgia, had been one of the first to experience the effects of the mortgage meltdown. As with all of the companies that had bet on rising property values, it depended on a steady stream of new mortgage originations. By early 2008, quality originations were becoming scarce, and there was worry that this company would need to close completely. I worried that I would not be able to deal with yet another billing disaster.

In a surprising development, this client had made a partial payment in January. In February, I wrote a thank-you note to their internal lawyer, mentioning as I did in many of these notes that we relied on such payments to keep our own operations going in a difficult time. The note concluded with "I know we all very much want to help you."

A couple weeks later, this internal lawyer came to Los Angeles and insisted on taking my partner and me to dinner. In the overwhelming bustle of a busy steakhouse, he told me: "I've been an outside lawyer sending bills. I've been an inside lawyer, paying bills. I've done this for a long time. But I've never seen a note like that." As the evening wore on and drinks were served, he began to ask me very personal questions. For example, we covered my divorces in suitable detail.

On returning to Georgia, he wrote me an e-mail, worried that he had gone too far in his questioning. A couple months earlier, I probably wouldn't have replied, but now I wrote back, letting him off the hook, telling him I enjoyed dinner and sounding an odd note that reflected the new way I was starting to look at my life:

> *Hopefully I am looking back at my variegated experiences with humor, and appreciation for the good in life. From that perspective, I can enjoy even the setbacks.*

In March, another payment—for $26,000—arrived from this client.

A few days later, I sat in the waiting room of the large corporate real estate firm that had represented us in our tiny lease negotiations. From the floor-to-ceiling window on the fortieth floor, I surveyed the vast expanse of Los Angeles as if I were in a spaceship. Our new landlord was finally ready to sign the lease that we had signed weeks ago.

This was the moment of truth—our first payment of rent plus a security deposit. I handed over a cashier's check—for $23,450. I did not have to liquidate my retirement account. I had been grateful for a good client I already had. Now I had the deposit I needed. The moving trucks arrived at our old offices the next morning. We had a new office, with room to work well and room to grow. Unlike Bear Stearns, our little firm lived on.

CHAPTER 10

Mediation

By March there had been no movement toward the resolution of my marital separation stalemate.

Still, I was determined not to use the adversarial legal process to force an end to the marriage. I had seen and felt the damage this would cause when my first marriage ended. California's "family law" courts provide a forum where families can burn their bridges and their money, where they can express sentiments and take positions that will destroy their relationships with their children and their children's well-being. I did not want to go there.

I felt helpless, and to blame. How had I done this? After four years, I could not find any way to unwind what I had done when I left. My old closet no longer had room for my clothes. There were two new dogs in the house, and I was not sure I liked them. I began to watch for something for which I could feel grateful. My ex had given me a Christmas present, one of Robert B. Parker's Sunny Randall novels. But there was too much anger in my heart. A Christmas present thank-you note was not going to be enough to heal it.

What could I praise and be thankful for with true conviction? What would recognize that something good and valuable remained between us? Surely, my ex was bound to do something I found right? But from my twisted viewpoint, I could see little for which I should be thankful.

Then, on my daughter's eighth birthday, her mother threw her a party. The site was well-chosen and unique. There were clever games, and plenty of cake and pizza. Each of the girls went home with several individual pieces of art that they had not thought themselves capable of doing. It was the first party to which my daughter had invited only girls. My little girl was growing up, and through her mother's diligence, this had been recognized and appropriately feted. I could find nothing cynical to say about this lovely party. So I wrote a thank-you note:

Thank you for taking the time to make the arrangements for our daughter's party. It looked like a lot of fun, and I think she really appreciated having some control over the theme. The invitations were very classy too.

Whether this thank-you note made a difference at all in the way my ex thought, I can't say. But something within me changed when I wrote it; the note made a difference to me.

Soon after, we met with a mediator. After a few minutes, the opposing positions were on the table, and there was heartbreak in the words we heard from each other. The mediator listened patiently to our differences and began gently guiding us to an agreement. Sometimes the mediator ignored our attempts to deviate down hurtful, unproductive roads. At other times, she sympathized just long enough to let us know our pain was not unheard or unrecognized before turning back to the business at hand, an agreement. There were several days when success was truly in doubt. On one of these days, I wrote to the mediator to thank her for her patience and the way she used her experience to present solutions that had worked in the past and could work again. I told her that even if our case ended up in court, I would appreciate what she had done.

When we finally had an agreement, I wrote her another note:

As you know from my pained expressions or outright whining, there were times when I had despaired of any end to the process. Thank you for dealing with these feelings and all the other difficult issues presented and keeping the process moving. You are doing good work, and increasing peace in the world.

She wrote back to say it was an honor to work with us.

Perhaps my thank-you notes had little to do with the fact that the mediation process worked. In any case, in the ensuing year, I found more things to appreciate about my ex-wife and wrote more thank-you notes. Either she reacted to the thank-you notes by doing a lot more things that I could appreciate, or she had been doing things that I should have been appreciating all along.

CHAPTER II

Birthday Cards

On her birthday that March, I gave my daughter an electric piano.

A few months before, my mother had been hospitalized, and my daughter and I visited her in Cleveland. My daughter, bored without cable TV, had sat down at my parents' unused piano and started banging on it. My sister sat beside her then and started to show her how to play. They did not get up for an hour.

When we got home, my sister sent my daughter a box full of the music from underneath the piano seat and a letter of encouragement, with a drawing of a ballerina. With the help of a friend, I found an enthusiastic teacher, and I wrote thank-you notes to the friend and to my daughter's teacher. Yet, at first, I did not write a thank-you note to my sister. My older sister and I have not been close. I know this sounds ridiculous, but in my view, this started when I was about two; once, when I was walking past her on the swing set, she swung hard into me and broke my nose. Fifty years later, we barely talked.

But when you get to the point of buying a piano, it's time to say thank-you for the inspiration.

> *Thank you for sending the music from our childhood to my daughter. She loves the music you gave her from* The Sound of Music, *and she is writing her own version of "My Favorite Things." I was intrigued by your choice to send McCartney, which I probably still can't play after all of these years.*
>
> *Love*

My sister had also sent along the songbook from Paul McCartney's first solo album. This was the music I had been playing when I gave up the piano forty years before. At first I thought my sister was trying to remind me of the frustration that caused me to quit the piano, but when I started playing a little, my daughter began to request McCartney's "Junk,"

which was the one song I could still play, and we would sing
together:

> Buy! Buy!
> Says the sign in the shop window.
> Why? Why?
> Says the junk in the yard.

My sister and I talked later about the broken nose. She
remembered the events differently, and I may have been
wrong about them for all those years. Did I walk in front of
her, or did she swing out of her way to land a telling blow?
Who knows?

My sister and I have something new and better to talk
about now: my daughter's piano playing.

My own birthday is in April, and it's traditionally been
a day of discomfort and discontent—another year
passed with nothing tangible to show except new pounds
and new wrinkles. But the April of my thank-you note year
was different.

Throughout the years of separation in my marriage, my
sister-in-law had continued to be a friend. In a way that was

unique to her, on my birthday she would often write a cheery letter that stretched from one greeting card to the next, so that only on reading all of the cards, which arrived by separate post, would you understand her complete message. This year I realized that these cards deserved a response.

> *You have always been a good sister to me, and never more so than now. By continuing to make me feel accepted and valued in this difficult time, you have made all of our lives, but most especially my daughter's, better. If ever I can be there for you the way you have been there for me, please let me know.*

She came to Los Angeles a couple of weeks later for my daughter's first communion. When we said good-bye, she said simply, "You will always be my brother."

"And you, my sister," I replied.

Meanwhile, Grace and I had continued to write thank-you notes for little things we did for each other, or just to be thankful for the chances we had to be together—though often it was just once a week, or even less. Now, for my birthday, she wanted to give me something special, and age-appropriate: tickets to a Jackson Browne concert. She barely knew who Jackson Browne was, but she bought tickets for his concert at the elegant Bakersfield Fox Theater, which was built in 1930—it's even older than I am, even older than Jackson Browne.

Up in the balcony, Grace bravely tried to mingle with the fifty-somethings. The guy next to her was a superfan, his long gray locks tied back in a ponytail. He had been to more than one hundred Jackson Browne concerts and raptly described the time that Mr. Browne had recognized him when they were both waiting in line for airline tickets. Grace asked if she could switch seats with me.

Jackson Browne was playing without a band; this was his solo acoustic tour. He walked onto the stage with a bit of stiffness, but his gray was dyed away, his voice and playing had improved over the years, and he had a nice, sardonic rap that explained his songs and allowed him to work with the bellowing stoners who never stopped requesting obscure parts of his songbook.

Around us, other fans were also showing their age. Our superfan informed us that there was one song that Mr. Browne never sings—it is about his first wife. Trouble was, superfan though he might have been, he couldn't remember the name of the song. Throughout the concert, everyone around us stumbled as we tried to remember it. Every once in a while, someone would try to sing a line of the song for the rest of the group, but we were a bunch of old people who could no longer remember even the name of a song we had sung a thousand times a year in our youth. Finally, when Mr. Browne broke into "Running on Empty," I was reminded of the drunken fan who shouts out the name of this song in the crowd noise that opens up that album: "Ready or Not!" I yelled, and all of us oldsters high-fived.

On the long freeway drive home from Bakersfield that night, Grace asked me the name of my favorite Jackson Browne song. "Fountain of Sorrow," I said. "But sometimes it's too sad to hear." In the joy of the moment, however, I could brave this sadness, and we listened to it a couple of times that night while riding through the emptiness along Highway 99.

Dear Grace,

   What a tremendous surprise to go to Bakersfield for my birthday and see Jackson Browne. Thank you for making my fifty-third birthday so special. You have made my fifty-third year one to remember and to be grateful for every day. I am so thankful for your love.

By 2007, it had been more than seven years since I had seen my college roommate, Neil, though I did try to at least make an effort to call him each year on his birthday, which is Halloween. Then, in April 2008, a few weeks before my birthday, Neil reached out to me.

Shortly after I turned seventeen, I left the tiny high school where I knew everyone and went to college at the University of Michigan, Ann Arbor, a small city artificially swelled by thirty-five thousand undergraduates, and roiling with the wreckage and excitement generated by remnants of the explosion of crazy ideas in the sixties.

At Michigan, I was given a student number. My number did not command very much respect. It seemed to mathematically ensure that I would be at the end of the line for everything. I was lost and I was scared. I missed my friends from high school, who had been everything to me.

I was also withdrawn and shy from shame over uncontrollable acne and an adolescent spinal deformity called Scheuermann's disease, in which the vertebrae grow unevenly, causing a kind of hunchback. I could tell myself the acne would eventually go away, but the prospect of life as a hunchback felt unbearable. I lived each day with the conviction that I was ugly and repulsively unlovable.

When I was in high school, I had relieved this anxiety by running on the cross-country and track teams, but at Michigan, the only thing that seemed to give me rest from my fears was drinking. Alcohol numbed my overwhelming fear and self-disgust. With a few drinks in me, I was recklessly in love with any girl, and any girl was the most beautiful woman in the world. The first time this happened, I was in a cab, and the girl was nearly thirty years old (ancient to me at seventeen). For a few minutes, I felt I really knew what love was at last. Then I passed out.

I was more than willing to let the drinking thing go too far. Several times, I ended up in the snow outside our dorm in my underwear, not knowing how I got there. I remember the confusion of waking up in the snow and observing, as if from outside my body, that I was cold. My concern was detached. I could have stayed there in the snow. Some nights I wanted to. With hangovers came a deeper depression, which lasted until the next drink.

I can write this today because I was rescued from these attempts at self-destruction by friends who cared. Nearly everyone at Michigan was older than I was, and most brushed by without seeing me. But a few of these older, more worldly young people decided to become interested in the vast drama of my life—which I was willing to spin for them after a few drinks. They were big brothers and sisters to me. They gave me a nickname, Doc, because I was taking premed courses even though I didn't want to be a doctor. They still call me that today. Doc, my old Michigan friend Dinah tells me, was a person who seemed to always live life out of duty, a duty he did not want. She knew Doc didn't want to be a doctor. She wasn't so sure he wanted to be a lawyer either.

Dinah and my other Michigan friends talked to me,

listened to me. They noticed when I was missing and pulled me out of the snow and off the bathroom floors where I passed out. They watched out for me. They made me feel that I was not alone.

Their friendship was the force in my life that made me decide to get my cold, drunken body up out of the snow and go back inside the dorm. I knew they would notice if I was not around the next day. Though they may not have appreciated it at the time, they saved my life.

None of them more than Neil. In the free-love ethos of the early seventies, limiting oneself to one woman at a time was considered quaint, at least to young men. Neil's magnetism was such that the women who dropped by his room were also willing to consider this idea quaint. A couple weeks into my sophomore year, Neil's roommate moved out, and he took me in with the understanding that there would be many nights when I would pick up the signal (in those days you'd hang a tie from the door) that I would be sleeping across the hall.

Neil is now a senior district attorney in a western state. In 1973, he was only a few inches taller than I was, but he seemed to tower over me. He was like no one I had ever seen, a godlike figure. His parents were Chinese; his haircut and his manner made him wholly American. He was from New York, but he spoke with the unaccented earnestness of the West. Tall, muscularly athletic, outgoing, funny, and charming, he had an energy that went on all night at parties. Sometimes, after everyone else had passed out, he would stay up painting the walls of the dorm hallways with his rendition of seventies album covers from such groups as Jethro Tull, Pink Floyd, and Yes, all while blasting the music from the vinyl inside the album covers. The murals were so good that the dormitory authorities paid him to paint more. These and other antics attracted many, many women.

With the eagerness of a groupie, I'd jumped at the chance to be Neil's roommate. I figured I would actually meet women, which at the time, of course, was the meaning of life. As pathetic as it seems in retrospect, I might not have spoken freely with women until I was in my twenties had it not been for the experience of talking to the women who dropped by to see Neil.

In April 2008 though, when Neil called me, he was not calling about my birthday. Birthdays are not his thing. No, he said, he was calling because he had been worrying about me.

"You didn't sound too good when you called last year," he said. He had been worrying that something was seriously wrong and that I was sinking into a depression like the one he had seen me through at Michigan. He was calling because he had decided that I needed to do something to keep from sinking deeper into the blues, and that the something would be running the Los Angeles Triathlon with him in September 2008.

On April 17, 2008, I wrote Neil a thank-you note:

> *Thank you for inviting me to work out for a triathlon in*
> *September. I will try. I just wanted to tell you how much I*
> *appreciated the friendship and the thought that you were*
> *thinking of me and wanting to take me out of my funk of last*
> *year. Here's hoping we run one in our nineties.*

Notice that I stopped short of accepting his invitation
to do the triathlon.

As soon as he received my note, Neil wrote back. He
shared that he had suffered through depression in his late
thirties. He had been losing his hair, a process he had been
unable to stop, and felt stuck in a rut in his job. His response was to become a triathlete.

> *My back was sore, my knees ached, and I felt as if the*
> *inevitable physical deterioration was playing havoc with my*
> *mental attitude. That fall I went to Hawaii and coincidentally*
> *enough flew in on the day of the Ironman Triathlon in*
> *Kona. Our hotel was on the race route. I saw guys much*
> *older than I was at the time looking like steel rebar, pounding*
> *the pedals and running. It hit me like a ton of bricks that I*

was responsible for my own welfare and couldn't blame it on nature. So I started to swim and bought a bike and started doing sprint triathlons. By virtue of cross-training, as hard as it was initially, my knees stopped aching, my back stopped hurting, my cardiovascular fitness improved."

Neil explained that pudgy and middle-aged as I was, I could do the same thing.

I just thought I'd 'pay it forward' especially since we go way back. All it takes is the first step and some encouragement. Only you can make choices to make you happy, no one else can, and I have learned you must choose to dwell in the present, appreciate what you have, and move forward. Hit the POOL and splurge and buy a decent road bike!

For me, Neil's response had special meaning. My hero, someone whom I had always felt was on a different, higher level, had opened up to me about his weakness in order to help me with mine.

Now all I had to do was buy some new running shoes. Maybe a bathing suit. And a decent road bike. What were the chances I would ever really do a thing like that?

CHAPTER 12

Doctor Hudson's Secret Journal

In March 2008, I took my daughter skiing for the first time. Thanks to the advice of Dinah, one of my University of Michigan friends, we stayed in a nice hotel with a Jacuzzi and a pool. After the first exhausting day of skiing at Big Bear, my daughter was, of course, not exhausted in the least, and insisted we go out to the heated swimming pool—an irresistible contrast with the freezing air.

A young father whose children were playing with my daughter was sitting with his wife in the Jacuzzi as it blew clouds of steam into the frigid winter air. From my place in the pool, I soon realized he was deep in conversation with his wife, explaining the surgery he had been scheduled for the next week. The operation, he said, sounded extreme and involved five incisions. He was afraid.

I knew what he was talking about.

In my mid-twenties, soon after I started work as an attorney, agonizing pains in my chest began to occur every night. I woke up choking on stomach acid and couldn't get back to sleep. My esophagus was a free-flowing two-way street—as many things as went down came back up. I remember the panic the first time I felt the acid cutting off my airway and the burning as it ran through my nasal passages.

So I started sleeping on the couch—a bad sign for my first marriage, which was less than a year old. One of our wedding gifts had been a long couch with pillows into which I could wedge my arms, propping myself into a sitting position. That is how I slept. For the next sixteen years.

Finally, my gastroenterologist, seeing the worsening of a condition called Barrett's esophagus and then a growing patch of dysplasia, a precursor to cancer of the esophagus, recommended me for surgery.

The procedure was called a Nissen fundoplication, a procedure that wraps part of the stomach around the esophagus to create a new valve that will hold food in the stomach.

It was this same operation that the man in the Jacuzzi was describing to his wife.

My principal recurring thought from this operation was that I never wanted another one. I woke up from the surgery terrified by the pain, unable to breathe correctly, and pinned down by tubes. In my mind, I was never the same after that. A follow-up operation was necessary to redo the stitches, leaving me feeling slower still.

But sitting in the hot tub at Big Bear, a frightened young man was describing the same pain I had been in before my surgery. Although I don't usually get involved in other people's conversations, on this occasion, I felt I had something to offer. Dressed as I was in my bathing suit, I showed him my five scars. I related how my daughter sees me as a person with an extra belly button due to the stitches that had to be redone.

I kept talking. As I went on, the formerly tragic story I had been telling myself all these years changed. I told him of how I now slept lying down. His eyes widened when I noted that now I could even sleep on my stomach. I could see how desperate he was for the pain to stop, how he longed to just once lie down and sleep next to his wife.

In that Jacuzzi I realized the magnitude of what I had been given: living the last ten years without pain. I should have been thankful for those traumatic days in the hospital. Here was yet another example of how I always viewed my life's troubles as a series of tragedies, which I survived only due to my Job-like patience and my Jesus-like goodness.

I should have been waking up every day of the past ten years with gratitude because I had been saved from another night of physical pain.

When I returned to Los Angeles after the ski trip, I wrote to the gastroenterologist, who had patiently followed my esophagus for nearly thirty years, watching its deterioration to a precancerous state, making sure I got the operation, and then following up with his endoscope to observe the healing and the disappearance of the dysplasia. My note said, "I should be thanking you for every night that I sleep without pain."

Locating my surgeon was a little more difficult, but eventually I found him at the University of Rochester Medical Center, in New York, where he was now Professor of Surgery and Oncology. I wrote thanking him for changing my life:

It has now passed about ten years since you did a Nissen fundoplication on me at the USC hospital. I met someone else recently who was considering the same surgery, and in explaining my progress, I was reminded of how grateful I should be for the last ten years, which have been free of the pain in my esophagus that so plagued me. Thank you for all you did for me then, and for so many others who have also been relieved of pain through your work.

A week later I was surprised when my surgeon took the time to write me back a letter of length and formality exceeding my own. In it, he said something that really struck me: "I do not often get long-term feedback from the patients, particularly when they are doing well, and I really enjoyed your note," he wrote. Like me, most of his patients were remembering only the pain, or complaining about something new. People who were doing well, well, they just never said anything.

There was one more doctor I needed to thank. Years ago, she noticed that something was seriously wrong. She had seen me twice within a few months, the second time to treat a flesh-eating bacteria that was eating my leg to the point where I couldn't walk. Instead of just handing out the Levaquin, she starting asking a lot of personal questions about what was happening in my life. I made all my excuses for the deterioration of my usually stubbornly healthy body—overwork, money problems, difficulty in my marriage. She wasn't buying it.

After running some tests to see what my liver looked like, she called me back in for a follow-up appointment. She shut the door. She told me it was time to clean up my act. I would need to take better care of myself. And I would need to stop drinking alcohol. Forever.

I tried to change her mind. Maybe I just needed a vacation. After all, it had been years since I'd had one. She kept repeating exactly the same words with which she began her speech: there were no compromises, no maybes.

Two weeks later, after seeking two second opinions, I accepted her simple diagnosis. I stopped drinking. Completely.

My birthday thank-you note to Grace had shown my gratitude for fifty-three years of life. It had not occurred to me before, but now that it had, I needed to thank the doctor who had made this possible.

Because my coverage had switched to Kaiser Permanente, my special doctor was not going to be covered by my insurance anymore. After returning for one last checkup, though, I wrote to her:

> *I can't believe the amount of time and the thoughtfulness and thoroughness of your work with me at the last checkup. Of course, I probably would not have been alive this year were it not for you. I am so grateful for all you have done to preserve my health over these years.*

While I'd waited for the bill after the last checkup in this special doctor's waiting room, I came across a tattered, yellowed paperback printed in the 1940s. It was lying on the table with the dog-eared copies of *People* and *Us*. The type was tiny, in the way of paperbacks of that era. It stood out from everything else on the table, decidedly out of place.

The book was *Doctor Hudson's Secret Journal* by Lloyd C. Douglas. I'd never heard of it. The introduction stated that the book was originally written by a doctor in a complex code that looked something like crazy Latin. The book purported to be "decoded and typed by a Robert Merrick assisted by Nancy Ashford."

I started to read *Doctor Hudson's Secret Journal* right there in my doctor's lobby. Dr. Hudson wrote of a "secret" that he discovered when, a year after the death of his young wife, he sought to put a stone on her grave and didn't know what to say on it. Walking among the stonecutters, he came across a sculptor in the process of completing the sculpture of a "triumphant angelic figure." The sculptor asked him if he had "victory."

"Victory over what?"

"Oh—over anything—everything."

Later, after reading the whole book, I would find that the actual words of the secret to everything are not revealed in it. I was drawn in, however, by the book's opening chapters in which the sculptor spoke of the "secret" with the breathlessness of a Tony Robbins or a writer of the many "secret" books that claim that positive thinking can attract positive events. As a result of the secret formula, the sculptor claimed, "I now have everything I want, and can do anything I wish! So can you! So can anybody! All you have to do is follow the rules! There's a formula, you know."

Reading just the opening pages, I decided that I definitely wanted to know the formula. I told the receptionist I wanted to borrow it and wondered if it belonged to the office.

"I don't know where it came from. I think someone just left it there."

"Do you mind if I take it?"

"No, go ahead."

Upon more detailed reading, it turned out that the "exact process for achieving power to do, be, and have what you want" is written on a single page torn from a Bible. The book never tells you what page of the Bible it is. But illuminated through the slowly developed melodrama of the book, it appears that the secret is to do good works, to give money away to the men and women in need around you. These are called "investments." They create a power that eventually brings you what is most important to you. This is never the money that you sent out, for to you, that investment is "all used up." It can be recovered only if the recipient forwards it to someone else. Then, just maybe, it will come back to you in a way you least expect but most need. These investments must be done in complete secrecy, and if they are mentioned or repaid, they lose their power. As the sculptor advised Dr. Hudson:

> "You will see that it has to be done with such
> absolute secrecy that if, by chance, the contact is not
> immediate and direct—if, by any chance, there is a
> leak along the line of transfer—the whole effect of it
> is wasted! You have to do it so stealthily that even
> your own left hand—"*

Dr. Hudson's investments were not just directed to the obviously needy. He loaned $20,000 to an apparently wealthy businessman whom everyone in the hospital hated because he complained about a bill. Dr. Hudson, looking more closely, found that the man was in dire straits due to his arrogance and bad temper. With Dr. Hudson's investment of $20,000, however, the man turned around his business, and later bought Dr. Hudson's hospital for an outlandish sum, saying he needed to build an office building.

---

* This quote, with its abrupt ending, is probably a clue that the "secret" is in Matthew 6:3: "But when thou doest alms, let not thy left hand know what thy right hand doeth."

In this way, Dr. Hudson got what he most wanted and needed: a beautiful new hospital, called Brightwood.

I tore through *Doctor Hudson's Secret Journal*, then went to the bookstore to try to find a newer copy. The book, written in 1939, is long out of print, and there were no copies in the bookstore. It turned out, however, that *Doctor Hudson's Secret Journal* was a prequel to Douglas's *Magnificent Obsession*, written in 1929. *Magnificent Obsession* sold millions of copies during the Great Depression and was made into two movies, a 1935 version with Robert Taylor and Irene Dunne, which made some radical departures from the book, and a 1954 version starring Rock Hudson and Jane Wyman, which is really a remake of the previous movie and doesn't pay much attention to the book either. For example, neither movie mentions the actual secret journal, resorting to more visual devices to convey the "secret." There was also a television series, *Dr. Hudson's Secret Journal*, which ran for ten episodes in the fifties, starring John Howard. I found a couple episodes on the Web, and they show Dr. Hudson, like any good doctor of those days, compulsively improving his mental acuity through frequent puffs on a cigarette or pipe. The novel *Magnificent Obsession* is still in print, so I began to devour that, too.

Magnificent Obsession, though it was a huge best seller, was a more difficult read than *Doctor Hudson's Secret Journal* and is filled with quaint dialogue and improbable melodrama. As in *Pollyanna*, much of the action occurs outside the narrative itself, retold through choppy dialogue. The hero, Bob Merrick (played by Rock Hudson in the 1954 movie), is a young playboy who nearly drowns after he drunkenly falls out of his sailboat. Merrick is saved by a "resuscitator" rushed across the lake from Dr. Hudson's cottage. (CPR was apparently not in common use, and a large, ungainly device known as a resuscitator was needed to restart breathing. Fearing for his own health, Dr. Hudson had one in his lake house.) By "singular coincidence," Dr. Hudson goes swimming at the same hour, and, exhausted by a lifetime of good works as a brain surgeon at Brightwood Hospital, he drowns. Had the resuscitator still been available where Dr. Hudson installed it, on his side of the lake, he might have lived.

Burdened with the knowledge that his life has been saved at the price of Dr. Hudson's, Merrick sobers up and discovers and translates Dr. Hudson's secret journal. Inspired, he devotes his life to becoming a brain surgeon and continuing Dr. Hudson's "investments." After a series of additional singular coincidences, Merrick saves the sight of Dr. Hudson's widow (played by Jane Wyman in the movie) and marries her.

As the reader may remember, one of my chief problems in 2007 was the nonpayment of a large legal bill incurred by clients who were at war with each other. Through my thank-you notes to good clients and the hard work of the others in my law firm, my practice was returning to profitability. But this troublesome and extremely large bill remained outstanding, and it ate at me. I felt I had done excellent work for these clients and put up with their internecine feuds longer than anyone else would have. If they had just paid their bill kind of sort of on time, all of the financial anguish I had been experiencing would not even have occurred. The money was available to them; indeed, I had recovered it for them.

At times, these clients would hint at a settlement of their differences, and as part of that, imply that the bill would be paid. Acting out of professional pride, I continued to recover monies for them during the period of dispute. Surely, I thought, they would recognize the value of my services. I would dream of how the money would allow me to breathe a sigh of relief, and maybe even take some time off. But the payment was never made, and it became clear that the clients intended to cooperate only to the extent necessary to dispute my bill.

One of these clients, in a tense exchange, accused me of being "disingenuous." This word is used by lawyers when they mean to call someone a liar, but want to do it with a stylish disdain. He had dealt with enough lawyers to know how to use it. It's a little like saying "with all due respect," which is what lawyers say when they don't respect you at all. Because I pride myself on truthfulness, this insult really upset me.

These clients began discussing a plan to pay my bill by assigning to me a part of a claim they had against a supposedly successful personal injury attorney in the San Diego area. This attorney had agreed he owed an extremely large sum of money to my clients, and further agreed he would pay it back at an extremely high rate of interest. He had even agreed that a judgment could immediately be entered against him for repayment of the loan. The amount owing was greater than the amount of my bill, so my clients felt I should be more than willing to accept part of the collections from this account in settlement of my bill.

I wanted no part of this arrangement, and the fact that the clients suggested it made me madder still. Then I did further research into the attorney and found that his license had been suspended. There was very little chance that he would ever pay the money back. He had fallen on hard times because his young adult daughter had become depressed, even suicidal. He had dropped his practice for months and moved to Nevada to support his daughter. Then his wife took ill, and he had to care for her as well. As he stayed away from his practice, and his financial desperation grew, he did what truly desperate lawyers sometimes do—he borrowed from the funds he held in trust for his clients. This is a big no-no. Although he had quickly paid the funds back, the damage had been done, and a suspension of his license was almost mandatory.

Instead of getting mad because he obviously could not repay the money, I was touched by this lawyer's story. It sounded so like the stories of hard times from the Great Depression related in *Doctor Hudson's Secret Journal* that I began to think I had found the book just because I should consider his situation in this light. These were exactly the type of down-on-your-luck men and women that Dr. Hudson sought out because he looked at them as "investment" opportunities.

I felt that I, too, was being called to make an investment. The same force behind the voice that told me to be grateful for what I had now had put this worn-out copy of the out-of-print *Doctor Hudson's Secret Journal* in front of me so that I would help this lawyer.

So I stopped complaining about the assignment of the receivable. Instead, I insisted that the entire receivable be assigned to me. The dispute with my clients was quickly settled, and I received the claim against the lawyer in addition to a fraction of what I was owed.

After the settlement was final, I phoned this personal injury lawyer. Before he could say anything, I told him I was canceling the liens that were keeping him from borrowing working capital. I told him that I was canceling the interest on the loan and that he could pay me without interest when he felt he was back on his feet.

The anger that had been in my heart over this unpaid bill had been hurting me, not the clients. They felt no shame at not paying. My anger was keeping me from moving on with more productive parts of my life. The true answer to my problems was in caring for the good clients I had, and the good people in my firm, not in immersing myself in this irretrievable situation. Once I made the choice to accept this settlement, my anger was gone, and I could move on to focus on these more important, more positive fronts.

I was learning that it was the hatred in my heart, not the hatred others held for me, that could truly destroy me. *Doctor Hudson's Secret Journal*, my newest inspiration, stressed the need to eliminate such anger before attempting new investments, and this part of the formula seemed to work as well as the rest.

I heard from my warring dissatisfied clients a year later and they were still fighting. Nothing had been resolved, and the money they saved by shortchanging me had been eaten up by successions of new disputes. Having moved on, I felt sorry for them. Although the San Diego lawyer made only a few token payments, the settlement had been a good one for me.

As on New Year's Day, I had listened to an inspiration. It seemed to be the right thing. As on the night that my daughter and I began to read *Pollyanna*, I had read a book that I would have disregarded had I found it in any other year. Once again, I chose to read, rather than look down on, the popular prose of another era. And it seemed to be the right choice.

I'm usually a logical person. Now I was following inspirations. At times I felt a little kooky, but it did seem to be working for me.

I made a few other investments after reading *Doctor Hudson's Secret Journal*. In keeping with his formula, I will not share them here.

I was sitting at the counter of Pie 'n Burger when I finished reading *Magnificent Obsession*. I also had *Doctor Hudson's Secret Journal* with me, as I would occasionally refer between the two while reading. Kathleen, a waitress at Pie 'n Burger, asked me what I had been reading so avidly. I explained to her how I had found *Doctor Hudson's Secret Journal* in my doctor's office, and how it had seemed to speak to me. Kathleen is a good waitress, and she appears interested just by the fact you are ordering another cup of coffee, but on this occasion I thought there was something extra-genuine in her interest. So I said, "Here, I want you to have these books."

"Thanks," she said. "I'll get them back to you when I'm done."

"No," I said. "I think the way this works is that you pass them on to someone else. And tell them to keep it a secret."

A year after switching from my special doctor for insurance reasons, I wrote her another thank-you note.

After all, I had another year for which to be grateful. Then she called. She had just given another attorney the same speech she had given me years earlier. Would I talk to him?

Having received my thank-you note, she knew I was doing well. She thought I could help.

CHAPTER 13

Extreme Thank Yous

Yes, it did get a bit ridiculous.

By the end of June, I had written 168 thank-you notes. As I struggled to keep up a pace that would have me writing 365 notes in a year, I started writing thank-you notes that no etiquette book in the universe would require or suggest. I began to think of these as extreme thank yous.

I tend to misplace and forget things: my wallet, cell phone, iPod, briefcase, keys. (One day, after tossing drawers and closets and heaving couch pillows in a raging last-minute search, I found my cell phone in a pile of wet laundry, causing my daughter to remark: "Keep your eye on that thing because it literally has legs.") So I started writing thank-you notes to the restaurant manager at Souplantation, the hotel security officer at the Biltmore in Arizona, and all the others who found my things and returned them to me. Even when people were a bit skittish about giving me their name, as was the attendant who helped me find my wallet in California Adventure's Hyperion Theater, I would take extra time to be sure they understood my gratitude for how they had gone above and beyond.

One day, I found a $10 bill tucked neatly under my front door. It had dropped out of my pocket, and my neighbors, instead of figuring they must have dropped it themselves or that it was their lucky day, had realized that the money belonged to the only other person in an apartment in that stairwell. So I wrote them a note thanking them for returning the $10 and letting them know how grateful I was to have such good and honest neighbors.

I may be absentminded, but I am not unlucky. I am a lucky man.

While they may have been examples of overdoing it, extreme thank yous had their own rewards. The act of writing them focused and calmed me. Just making my to-do list of thank yous showed me that I had a lot to be grateful for. And writing the notes themselves gave me a growing sense that my life was not so bad after all. Often I remembered wonderful things that these same people had done the year before or, in some cases, for most of the years of my life, though I'd never written them a thank-you note for any of it before. My parents, to take one example.

The extreme thank yous had started with Scott at Starbucks, and when Scott left, a young woman named Kimber started working there and *she* started remembering my name. Maybe Scott told her it was a good idea. So I wrote Kimber a note, much like the one I had written to Scott.

Kimber came to me the next time I saw her with tears in her eyes. She had spent years, she said, studying and working in the service industry. Although she had just earned her degree, she was beginning to doubt this choice. She provided service that could make her professors proud, and she worked hard at it every day, delivering the Starbucks coffee experience in the optimum way as she had been taught, which included learning people's names and treating them like people. Yet no one had ever taken the time to write a thank-you note to her before.

Then there was the courtroom clerk. We'll call her Sherry.

As a litigation attorney, I deal frequently with courtroom clerks. They are the gatekeepers to the judge. If your papers don't get past the clerks, the judge never sees them.

The papers can arrive on the judge's desk carried by someone who is bored and rolls his or her eyes in comment on your arguments, or they can be delivered with a look that implies that perhaps a legitimate request has been made.

Some courtroom clerks are a bit overcome by their small amount of power, some are worn down by the pressures of the attorneys and the judge, some are just fed up by the realization that each new person has the same senseless dilemma as the last person. Many clerks have a manner that conveys a sort of contempt: "I don't know why your client is paying so much for an idiot like you. Even I'm smarter than you."

During my thank-you project, I needed to go to a downtown court department that handles attachments. Legal attachments are often emergencies, and plaintiffs often panic about them because the attachment may be the last chance to glom on to some compensation. Defendants can be equally frantic, as they are about to have their last remaining assets seized by a creditor. The clerk in this department, Sherry, dealt with the attorneys calmly, professionally, and even-handedly. She spoke to all the attorneys as if we were worthy of respect—even if our papers were not exactly right and needed some corrections. She required corrections, but only when they mattered substantively. I did not always get everything I wanted in the department where Sherry presided, but I always felt that I was listened to.

After one of my cases had been heard in Sherry's court-room, I decided to send her a note:

>*Thank you for your professional manner and even-handed courtesy to the attorneys who come to your department. It can't be an easy job, but it is much appreciated by those of us who appear there.*

When I next appeared in this department, Sherry came up to me in front of my associate and thanked me for the note. She said she had saved it and looked at it from time to time in order to "cheer herself on" during the difficult days— "and there are quite a few of them."

L ooking for places to express gratitude also inspired me to thank my daughter's teacher after one of our parent-teacher conferences. Parent-teacher conferences can be nerve-racking for me. While my daughter's conferences are predominantly, and sometimes overwhelmingly, positive, like most parents, I have a hard time hearing of any imper-fection.

The first parent-teacher conference of my thank-you note year was no less nerve-racking, and it seemed to last an agonizingly long time. When it was over, though, I reflected on the level of detail that had been provided by the teacher and how she had recounted incidents involving my daughter with specificity and anecdote. Whether I agreed or disagreed with her assessments, I had to admit that they involved a great deal of care. So I wrote:

> *Thank you for taking time out of your schedule, over and above the usual, to spend time with us discussing our daughter. You went into such depth and detail that it was evident how much care you have devoted not just to her intellectual progress, but to her emotional development as well.*

This teacher looked at me differently after that. First of all, she remembered me. Whether she had ever looked at me with a skeptical or adverse judgment before that I am not sure, but I am nearly certain that she didn't after that note was written. By noticing how she truly cared about my daughter, I had convinced her that I, too, cared, and now we had something special in common.

One day Amy, who cuts my hair, seemed in actual need of a thank-you note.

Usually when you arrive for an appointment with Amy, she greets you with open arms and a stream of mysterious New Age advice in breathless Spanglish that leaves you laughing. Her clothes are loose and soft, and her body moves around the chair in a warm cloud as she cuts your hair. One day in 2008, though, Amy was subdued, and her voice was filled with resignation. She seemed almost tight-lipped. So I asked what was up, and she said, "To tell you the truth, John, I am thinking of giving this up. I don't think I can do this work anymore. I just don't know what I am doing."

Knowing the pain of feeling misplaced in middle age, I wrote a note to her that night:

> *Thank you for all the wonderful work you have done with cutting my hair. It really lifts my spirits to talk to you and to come out looking better. You may be thinking of changing your life-work, but please know you do good work right where you are now.*

I was afraid that when I next called, she would not be there, and I wanted her to know how much I truly appreciated the way that she made me feel good for a couple of hours during what was often, otherwise, a rocky week.

When I came back for my next haircut, Amy's mood

had brightened. She thanked me for my note. Although the salon was closing down, Amy had changed her mind about quitting the business.

"I was so happy to get your beautiful note," she said. "It made me realize why I like this work. I am here for you and for my other clients. That is why I do what I do."

Even today, Amy brings up my thank-you note. Every time I see her she introduces me as "John, my wonderful friend, who wrote me that beautiful letter I was telling you about." Of course, there are other reasons for Amy to be happier. She got married. She has taken more time for vacations. She now works in a bustling salon surrounded by a crowd of her customers.

Still, she saved my note. She told me, "When people come over, my husband says, 'Amy, show them this wonderful letter.'" She has returned to her former happiness and continues to dispense life advice from her unique New Age perspective. She is thinking of running for mayor of Los Angeles and in California, which she pronounces "Callyfornia," a bit like Governor Schwarzenegger, her candidacy could be viable. "You will vote for me?" she asks. Of course, I say.

By June, after writing 168 notes, I was receiving unsolicited phone calls, hugs, and e-mails, but also a lot of thank-you notes. In fact, more thank-you notes than I had ever received in my life. By this time, I was very focused on the act and the art of writing thank-you notes, and I admired many of the ones I was receiving. I began to save the thank-you notes, e-mails, and letters. I cherished and cared for them. Each thank-you note became a valued collector's item to me. Looking through the notes I received became as calming as looking through my list of notes written.

Some people wrote that the power of the thank-you note in their lives had led them to write notes to others. Others remarked that writing such notes was helping them to get bills paid. One of my favorite notes was the tiny one that I received in my clean laundry from a woman at the Drop a Load Laundromat; she made her living by helping with the fluff-and-fold service I used. Writing on the back of the Laundromat's business card, Jessica told me: "This is a little note to thank you! For always being such a wonderful customer. Thanks so much. By Jessica. —Hope you like everything!"

CHAPTER 14

The Unopened File

We liked our new offices on Lake Avenue, the principal north-south street in Pasadena's center. Our biggest banking client had offices directly across the street. The lawyers' offices extended around the periphery of the space, so every one of those offices had windows. From some of the windows, you could see the beautiful San Gabriel Mountains, where I had walked in January.

My "office"—or perhaps I should say my desk—sat out in the empty space in the middle of all the offices. Next to me was the desk of my beloved paralegal. I was surrounded by shelves and boxes of papers, but basically I was on display. Our meetings were held in the open air of this space.

I was totally accessible, and everyone came up to me constantly. Everyone in the office could see my face at all times. They could hear everything I said on the telephone, and they could sense any tenseness in my voice. When I seemed displeased, there was no need for rumors about it. They could hear me laugh, if something was funny.

In June, three months after our move, some of the boxes surrounding me still had not been unpacked. Some of the stuff in these boxes was personal, collected from all the office moves that had preceded this one. Because these files were not needed, they were not unpacked.

With her boundless energy and intolerance for disorganization, my paralegal would attack these boxes in her spare time, finding the place where each item or file could belong and be available if ever needed. In her diligence, she came upon an old Redweld file of holiday cards and letters. It contained some cards or letters that were more than twenty years old. Hungry for more gratitude, I looked to find some in this old file.

The first thing I notice when I look at this file today is that, though it is decades' worth of keepsake papers, it is smaller than the file of thank-you notes and e-mails I saved from my thank-you note project. It does contain letters of thanks from paralegals and others who had worked with me over the years, and some letters of gratitude from clients who hadn't been able to pay. One letter of gratitude, dated 1986, was the only letter from a paying client from my first fourteen years of law practice. I had probably received other thank-you letters, but what remained were the few that had been saved by someone who had found such things on my desk. Apparently the red folder had filled up as my desk was swept for each move. I'd never stopped to review it before.

Inside, I found a number of uncashed checks for $100 or $200 from some of my pro bono clients. I had dismissed these efforts to pay as meaningless in view of the actual bill, or what the actual bill would have been had I sent it. Rather than accept these amounts, I had tossed the checks in a drawer or into this red file, uncashed. Symbols of my pride. A pride that had nearly brought me down.

Despite the painstaking work necessary in my practice to save every last bizarre expression of hatred from opposing attorneys and their clients, I had done little over the years to save the letters of gratitude that people had written me. And the gratitude of my nonpaying clients was not all I had discarded in this Redweld file.

In the same folder, I found a pink envelope. On it, in red ink, were the simple words *My Husband.* I recognized the handwriting of my first wife, from whom I had been divorced for twenty-one years.

My first wife was not a writer during our time together.

She did not write many letters or notes to me or to anyone else. When she bought a card, it had to say exactly what she wanted it to say. She did not add to it or qualify it or adjust it. It would usually just be signed with her first name, sometimes under the word *Love*. In this case, the only way I now knew the envelope came from her was that I could recognize that the words *My Husband* were in her handwriting. When I opened the envelope, twenty-one years later, there was nothing, not even a signature. The message of the card was simple: "Let me love you."

I may not have read this at the time. If I did, I did not get the message. I know that I never responded.

I did read it in my thank-you note year. Out there in the open at my desk. Where everyone could hear me laugh. And everyone could see me cry.

CHAPTER 15

Father's Day

My Father's Day gift from my younger son was a thank-you note:

Thanks . . . and thanks again!
For stepping up for me.
Happy Father's Day
Thanks for providing hope.

Earlier in June, he had been detained by a police department when he went in to pay his parking tickets. Generally, I believe he should handle his own legal problems. But this was a case of mistaken identity, and that caused me to react with a protective streak that he had not seen in me for a while. I refused to leave the police station until I could leave with him. My son was a bit surprised, because I had been more distant of late, trying to make sure he learned to take responsibility for his actions. But writing so many thank-you notes had caused me to assess what I could be grateful for in having a son. An unusual number of friends of mine had lost their young sons and daughters to drugs or alcohol or self-destruction. Taking stock of many things, and thinking about this son, I decided to be grateful for every day he was alive and for every day there was another chance for him to discover his place in the world, a task that seems so peculiarly difficult for this generation.

CHAPTER 16

A "Business" Trip to Beijing

In August, I stopped resisting my youngest brother's repeated invitations to visit him in China, purportedly to advise him on some legal matters. Although he was more than willing to pay for my time, and able to do so, in the past I had been unwilling to bill him. My pride as the older brother got in the way. But in August, my court dates slowed, and I was able to schedule the time to take my daughter with me and go. On China Eastern Airlines, flying to Beijing can cost as little as a poorly scheduled flight to New York. The food is a little unusual and the movies are all in Chinese, but I never watch the movies or eat the food on airplanes, anyway.

When we got to Beijing, it turned out that there was little legal work. Instead, my brother and his wife saw to it that my daughter and I attended the Olympic Games (where we saw Michael Phelps swim to two of his gold medals), toured the Forbidden City (where Chinese mothers found my daughter's appearance so unusual that they wanted to take pictures of her with their children), and climbed on the Great Wall of China (though, for my daughter, the real wonder of the trip was swimming with her young cousins in the "swimming pool," which was, in fact, a freezing stream outside my brother's home near Beijing).

My brother's staff treated us with great care, and I felt grateful to them for feeding my daughter, driving us around, and making sure we were comfortable. While recognizing that they would not understand a word of what I wrote, I still wrote thank-you notes to Xiao Bai, the driver; Cheng Ayee, the house boss; Xiao Feng, who took care of Mei Mei (younger sister); and Xao Wang, who took care of Di Di (younger brother). I wrote of the special kindness each had shown to us: driving us to the airport, combing out my daughter's hair, making sure she had food she could eat despite the culinary culture gap, doing the laundry. The laundry at my brother's house was especially magical. Wherever you discarded a towel or a piece of clothing (and you could discard them practically anywhere), they were mystically swept up. They reappeared, clean and folded, on your bed about an hour later.

Once I was back in California, I received a call and an e-mail from my brother in which he related how each of his staff had been honored by my notes and had insisted that he translate them word for word. If this had not been my thank-you note year, I would not even have taken the time to learn their names.

Writing the thank-you note to my brother, I reflected on how the process of writing the notes had caused me to belatedly recognize his kindness and generosity, not only to me and my daughter, but to my parents and other members of our family. My failure to be grateful to him, and to notice all he was doing, had left our accounts out of balance. By accepting and being grateful for his generosity, I felt a balancing of our books, a peace in my heart that allowed me to be closer to him.

I have five brothers and three sisters, each of whom is remarkable in his or her own way. I tried to find an opportunity to remind each of them of my admiration through the thank-you note project. Some of my brothers and sisters would drop everything and immediately travel thousands of miles to help my parents or other brothers and sisters. My brother who is a surgeon once flew to another brother's side when he was worried about chest pains and another time spent days reviewing my father's heart care. My brother in China flew to Cleveland to help supervise the after-care for my father when he had a heart attack. My sisters, who live in Seattle and Fairbanks, flew to Cleveland and then later to Florida to watch over my mother during several hospitalizations.

At fifty-three, I knew I was lucky to have such siblings, and I was lucky that all my siblings were alive. These were blessings I had seldom noticed until my thank-you note project, during which I wrote a thank-you note to each of my brothers and sisters. It was not hard to find something to say.

CHAPTER 17

Economic Meltdown on Lake Avenue

By the second half of what I had planned as my thank-you note year, two events seriously slowed, and nearly stopped, the writing of the notes. Although I didn't know it at first, these complications—and my reactions to them—were going to prevent me from completing 365 notes in a year. Because of these two events, the thank-you note year became the thank-you note project, with the time frame extended until I could compose all 365 notes, whenever that might be. These complications slowed me but they didn't stop me, and within fifteen months, I finished 365 notes. I would find I needed to write every single one of the 365 notes before the promise I had heard in the mountains would come true.

Before that could happen, however, the interrupting events nearly caused me to lose my way.

First, there was the banking meltdown. By July, the effects of this crisis could be seen right outside the front doors of our office building. Restive, impatient, fearful people lined up on Lake Avenue to withdraw their money from the bank that had its name atop two of the largest office buildings on the street. Between June 26, when a U.S. senator sounded an alarm about the solvency of the bank, and July 10, the line of frightened people on the street grew. The people in this line and on the phone and the Internet withdrew $1.3 billion from the bank during this short period. In one week, the bank laid off 3,800 people. And by July 10, the bank's stock, a bunch of which I'd bought at about $28 per share, was selling for $.28. On July 11, the bank was taken over by the Federal Deposit Insurance Corporation.

My firm had recovered by this time and was doing well, so this bank failure might have been something I could watch with detached sympathy—except that many of those 3,800 people were my friends. And the bank was my biggest client.

My first reaction to this crisis was to put additional discipline in my daily routine. The FDIC's takeover of the client occurred on a Friday, and after a weekend of worry and dire news reports, I decided the most important thing for me to do on Monday was to put on a suit. I don't wear suits anymore, except to court, where they are required. Yet on that dark Monday, and for several days afterward, I wore a suit. I was on display at my desk, and I wanted everyone to know that I was ready for the meetings that would come and that our work was proceeding, not breaking down.

In another respect, however, I did not handle this crisis well. I lost focus on my thank-you note project. Between July 10 and the end of the month, I wrote only one note. Maybe I was wondering about how I would replace a client that accounted for as much as 40 percent of our firm's revenue. Maybe I was worried about the next step in the dozen or so cases I was handling for the bank. Maybe I was worried about last month's bill, or next month's.

The one note I did write during this period was to an employee of the bank who took the time to call me and tell me that the books were closing, and if I had bills to submit, I better get them in promptly:

Thank you for alerting us regarding the need to get our bills in, and otherwise being so supportive of our efforts for the client. It seems that none of us can tell where this is all going, but in the midst of confusion and panic, genuine human caring stands out as a unique and invaluable treasure.

Many of the people around my friend were losing their jobs, and she would eventually lose hers too. In all of that, it was touching that she had some thought for us. Today, she works at a new company that became a new client of my law firm.

This bank meltdown was the first new crisis that had occurred in my professional life since the beginning of the thank-you note project. If I had been in the same state of mind I had been in at the end of 2007, the bank failure might have topped my list of the latest reasons my life really sucked. The thing was, in 2008, I didn't keep a list like that anymore. I had a new list: 170 things I should be grateful for.

My relative calm derived in part from the financial stability that had returned to our firm. Our bills were being paid largely on time. I was well aware of this because of the many thank-you notes I had been sending to the clients who were paying their bills.

Moreover, I had a good supply of new cases and new clients that had been developed just since the first of the year. In part, this happened because of the new practice I had begun in January of sending a thank-you note to the person referring the case, or to the client who entrusted us with it.

While I was sending out thank-you notes in January and February, I had focused on how at least some of my billing problems were attributable to my own poor client selection. I needed to select cases that were more appropriate to my own capabilities and the capabilities of my small firm. I had plenty of work, but not enough work from clients with reasonable expectations, clients who recognized that our work was necessary and needed to be compensated. On January 10, 2008, one of my colleagues sent me a case from such a client, and I wrote him the first of these notes:

Thank you for sending us the new matter. I am hoping that, with a little luck, we can keep the punitive damages under $1,237,506, the amount alleged. We appreciate your confidence in our venture.

This attorney sent me another case just like it later in January and several more throughout the year. I sent several more thank-you notes. He later told me he was happy to send me such cases, and that my notes reminded him to send me more. In their absence, he would have wondered, Did I already have all the good cases that I wanted?

I sent similar thank-you notes to the other lawyers who sent me good, paying cases during the year. In each case the attorney to whom I sent a note acknowledged receiving it with gratitude and sent me another good case soon after. At most, I invested an hour in the process of writing the thank-you notes for these referrals.

Because I was focused on writing the notes, I also was focused on whether the case was one that, in my best judgment, I should be thankful for, or one on which I should pass. Just as thank-you notes had focused me on who was paying, they had focused me on which cases I should be accepting.

In addition, the business of the firm had grown and diversified by July 2008, as the result of my decision to take on a partner. During 2007, Lois, who had been my friend for nearly thirty years, had started working for me on a part-time, hourly basis. It had been nearly two decades since we had worked together, and so I had forgotten some of the unique synergies that our personalities and approaches to litigation could produce. By the end of the year, I worried that I could no longer afford to pay her on time. I decided instead to make her a partner. This decision seemed counterintuitive, but only from my myopic view at the time. While I attributed this decision to financial insecurity, this was just another example of how I was failing to recognize the wealth my friendships set out right in front of me. My decision to make Lois a partner was the last, and perhaps the most important, piece in my economic recovery program. Responsible again to a partner, I began to be more responsible in my decision-making about the economic consequences of accepting certain cases. Lois took a leading role in my most difficult cases, sharing the burden of the cases' emotional elements, which allowed me to focus more successfully on their legal and factual issues. Throughout my thank-you note year, I wrote many thank-you notes to Lois.

Reading some of my e-mail from that period, I see that I did project calm to colleagues and clients, focusing on the things I could control and encouraging others to do the same. For example, to increase the visibility to other clients needing our firm's expertise, I wrote an article for the firm's Web site discussing a new mortgage law. My thank-you notes had given me a more balanced view of each day's events, no matter how extreme they seemed.

By July 2008, the financial devastation in our country was in full swing. Millions were out of jobs and wondering if the jobs would ever reappear. Things were bad again. They just didn't take me down with them.

The only real sign of distress was my failure to keep pace on the thank-you note project.

CHAPTER 18

Heartbreak

Grace and I had had a good year together, until October.

In the spring, I'd asked her to come along with me on a business trip to Phoenix. My work there was to evaluate properties involved in several of the mortgage frauds coming to light in Phoenix's luxury neighborhoods and to try to figure out who was behind the frauds.

Splurging with the insanity of someone who has no money, I'd booked us at the Biltmore, and when my business meetings and tours were over, Grace and I decided to take an extra day. With Grace there, I felt that I had a reason to take a whole day off. We roamed the gardens in our bathrobes. When people looked at us funny, we said, "Isn't that what these things are for?"

Grace was gentle and patient with me that weekend, as if her only reason for being was being with me. She did not think it crazy when I went out to buy a book on tape and a CD player because I needed to listen to something during my sleepless nights. She did not mind my anxiety over my cases. We joked about how very normal we felt together.

When we'd started out for Phoenix my hands had been swollen and deeply cracked with bleeding cuts from psoriasis, which was always made worse by the tension of my work and the worries about finances. But during this single day off, my hands began to heal, and by the time we boarded the plane to return to Los Angeles, all of the cuts had closed.

Dear Grace,

Thank you for coming with me to Phoenix. As you could tell, I needed some time off. Even more, I needed some time to be with you. However normal this time was—that

kind of normal was very, very good. As always, being with
you is healing for me. You could see it on my hands, but there
was also healing in my heart.

Love,
John

Then in April, she'd surprised me with the Jackson
Browne tickets for my birthday. And at the end of July, when
it had been a year since Grace and I had gone out for the first
time, she remembered our anniversary with a note:

I am so happy that you called me a year ago and asked
me to go on a date with you. You mean the world to me and
you bring so much joy to my life. I love you.

At the time I received this note, I had been consumed
with anxiety over the banking meltdown; the note made me
realize that I'd lost focus on what was now an important
part of my life.

So I thanked Grace for all the little things she had
done during the previous weeks to cheer up my apartment,
which, with the summer months, had become an inferno:

Thank you for the picture frame, the coffee—and all of the little things you have done to make this humble apartment a warmer place for my daughter, Brody, and me. It is your presence that most warms this place and makes it a treasured place of good memories.

I also thanked her for remembering our one year together, and for giving me a songbook to play on the piano.

Then, in October, she broke up with me.

I was driving uphill outside Pasadena when she called.

"I don't think we should see each other anymore."

"Okay."

I pulled over. Like any other Angelean, I talk on the phone while driving. But on this occasion I wasn't talking, yet still could not drive. I didn't know what to say. Grace's voice sounded strong, as if she'd been holding this back, and now she really had to say it.

"If that's how you feel, then I have to accept it."

"It is."

She sounded like someone who had been summoning the courage to say this. But she hadn't rehearsed the explanation, so we didn't say much after that. We had always been a bit awkward on the phone. Now there was nothing else to say.

I have tried at various times to keep a diary. I never do. But there's usually one around if I really care to make an entry. There is an entry for that day, which says: "Grace has broken up with me, and, it seems, this time, for good."

Grace called a few days after the breakup, on Sunday morning, a time when we were usually together. Her voice seemed lighter, as if a weight had been taken off her. She cheerily ran down her plans for the day. I tried to be pleasant, but found that I didn't feel any more competent than a high school boy in the art of "just being friends," an art the person deciding on a breakup expects to be so effortless.

I did tell her that I had been lying in bed missing her. I did not tell her that I had been surprised to find tears along my cheekbone when I got up to get the phone.

I found myself not understanding what went wrong. When things had been good between us, and they often were, I experienced a love that I had not felt before. With my concentration on gratitude, I had been able to appreciate this.

Looking back at our recent conversations for clues, though, I found enough. The strain of dating someone who could not seem to get his divorce finalized was beginning to show. I heard the observation: "Given that you're a lawyer, it would seem that you of all people could be divorced if you wanted to be." The strain of dating someone who was so obviously in love with his eight-year-old daughter was also showing: "It's really hard to compete with how happy being with your daughter makes you."

I understood these strains, and I could sympathize with them, but I couldn't seem to change them.

Then I heard the leading question: "So, you don't want to get married again for years and years?" And I had to reply honestly that I wasn't sure that I would feel I wanted to get married again, even years and years from now.

I probably should have recognized that breaking up was inevitable then, but I had left it to Grace to decide.

You think these things don't hurt after fifty, but I had already found out differently when Grace broke up with me the previous Christmas.

Throughout my thank-you note project, the person who had written me the most thank-you notes was the same person who wrote the first one, Grace. All of her notes were as lovely as that first one. She thanked me for making her birthday special, for the comfort of a loving heart, for making her feel loved, for the roses I brought her, for appreciating her, for gifts, for taking her on a trip, for framing a picture, for taking her to a concert, for taking the time to take her to the DMV and waiting while she renewed her license.

I had written Grace many thank yous as well. Beginning by thanking her for her Christmas present, I also thanked her for driving me to the airport and taking care of my cat and my apartment when I was away; for a travel diary; for taking me to the Jackson Browne concert; for buying me an Elton John music book when I mused carelessly about playing the piano again; for making my stuffy apartment pleasant with little vases, picture frames, and plants; for a beautiful lunch on the Fourth of July; for the memory of a beautiful morning together; and for buying me special note cards on which to write more thank-you notes. Although I had written many notes to Grace, she had written more to me.

Our thank-you notes so regularly provided more evidence of the validity of my grandfather's silver-dollar principle. By appreciating the things we did for each other, we encouraged each other to do more nice things. Which we then appreciated even more. The thank-you notes set out in my spreadsheet, or collected in my little file, summarized the special times we had. In between the thank-you notes we had a relationship, but the notes provided the admissible evidence I was always seeking.

Rather than destroy the good memories we had created together, I decided to try writing a thank-you note that showed that I was thankful for them, so that the last emotion I would feel in leaving this relationship was the thankfulness for the good things.

My next thank-you note would be the hardest of the 365 to write:

For discovering with me a way to go out on Saturday night and enjoy the night through the light in a loved one's eyes.

For the moments we spent together in the mornings.

For your laughter during our lunches at Subway.

For making me feel younger and better looking whenever I was with you.

For being my companion.

For giving me your true love.

For having the courage to give up something merely good because it was not what you truly deserve.

For all these things I am grateful. In thanks I will try to be your friend.

When I asked Grace whether she believed the thank-you notes made a difference in our relationship, she said, "They were really . . . separate." So they were. Whether we were together or apart, these notes are a separate record of moments and gifts, feelings that will never change. We can look back at concerts or trips, or mornings together, and still be grateful for what we had, rather than bitter about what we lost.

I have a note from Grace, also written in October:

I want to acknowledge that I love you and also let you know how important you are to me. You really need to know how wonderful you are because it is the absolute truth! Your patience overall and especially your patience with me is amazing—you consistently take the time to listen to me (or wait to eventually listen to me!) and help me see things more clearly. More importantly your love is unconditional and that is by far the greatest gift I have ever received.

Reading this note a year later, I could not figure out whether it was written before or after we broke up. So I asked her. It was written after. It was separate.

We were still friends. We still gave gifts to each other, though they were smaller and more infrequent. We still wrote thank-you notes. When Grace was laid off from a job, she resisted the temptation to wallow in a satisfying Johnny Paycheck "Take This Job and Shove It" reaction. Instead, she went home and wrote a thank-you note to the person who had given her the opportunity, expressing her gratitude for what she had learned. And that brought her peace.

Through our notes to each other, I learned to express and to accept gratitude in a relationship.

No matter how hard I tried to be grateful, though, I cannot deny that breaking up with Grace brought me down, and after that I wrote no thank-you notes for two weeks.

Until then, the good developments over the year had me believing I would be rescued from the depths I had experienced the previous year if I just kept writing thank-you notes. Yet when Grace called to break up with me, I felt like I was right back in the position that I had been in at the end of 2007. Despite hundreds of thank-you notes, wasn't I just reliving the end of my horrible year? Why hadn't my thank-you notes saved me from this disaster?

Bad things *were* starting to happen again, I thought.

I realized that I had trouble living without Grace. I wondered why I had not been a good enough person to see my way through this relationship. Or the two marriages that preceded it. Maybe I just plain wasn't good enough. The relationship stories in my life were always ending the same way because one of the two characters in the story was always me.

I could have thrown myself further into my work, but I had the sense I was already giving enough there. I could have rushed out to try to find another girlfriend, but truly I didn't want anyone else. I decided to take some time to figure out the real problem. What was the common denominator in all the failed relationships? Me.

There were many ways in which I needed to be a better person before I could feel I had a life that was good enough to share with someone else. I also had to admit to myself that I might never be good enough and might never succeed in a relationship. I had to admit I was probably one of those who were not suited to such things. I was now fifty-three and needed to accept reality. My daughter and my firm gave me a full life. Maybe that should be enough.

CHAPTER 19

The Stock Market Crashes . . . into Thanksgiving

Early every morning in October, I engaged in this ritual: I woke up, turned on the television, and clicked through CNN, FOX, MS-NBC. The political slant of the news channel made no difference. I was interested only in the Dow Jones Industrial Average. Slumped into my hammock-style Ikea chair, I kept hoping the market would finally hit bottom. It did not. The opening bell would ring on Wall Street, and the Dow would begin dropping like the pulse rate of a crashing heart patient. Surely, I thought, it would never sink below 12,000. Surely, it would never sink below 11,000. Surely, it couldn't go below

10,000, which would return it to the levels just after the September 11, 2001, attacks. Surely, it would never sink below 9,000. But it did. It sank and sank. And kept going.

I had no more stocks in savings, but I did have a retirement account. I created a conversion table in my head so I knew just how many thousands of dollars I was losing every time the market dropped a few hundred points, which it seemed to do right after I turned on the television each morning.

After each day's first wave of losses, I would take a shower. Then I would return to the television in my towel to see whether the bottom had finally been reached. A few hundred more points would be gone, and I would turn off the television. I did not need any more bad news that early in the morning. The turnaround would not be today.

A financial disaster movie was in the making. I'd been aware that the real estate market was inflated, but like most Americans, I had no idea that the country's venerable financial institutions and insurance companies had bet the life savings of their depositors and the careers of their employees on the bizarre proposition that anyone, literally anyone, was good for a million-dollar mortgage.

I felt stunned to realize that these sophisticated institutions, whose leaders earned millions in annual bonuses, had no backup plan except to ask a highly leveraged federal government for more leverage. And stunned to realize that the government had no better plan than to give this money to them. People speculated over which banks were "too big to fail." Then big names—very big names like Washington Mutual and Lehman Brothers—began failing. My money was in Citibank, which was rumored to be next.

Like the rest of America, I was realizing that our money had value based on the depositors' faith in the monetary system, and the banks had value based on the faith of the stockholders. If all that faith turned to fear, our money would disappear, along with the bank branch in the strip mall where I deposited and withdrew cash. Fear, not faith, was abroad in the land. I could feel the fear myself.

Then, out of the blue, the day before Thanksgiving, I received a thank-you note from a pro bono client I had helped twenty years before:

> *Hoping you all have the most Happy Thanksgiving. I always have you in my heart and I do my prayers every day and your name is always there, for health, for safety and needs, your work. I can never forget.*

I treasured this note, humbled by the strength of this woman's faith on the page.

Before the stock market crash, I had been getting better at seeing the world with less fear. That note, right before Thanksgiving, returned that less fearful lens to me. I could see, for example, that the largest asset I had in my law practice wasn't my skill, which had been sorely challenged, or my ideals, which I'd felt had been so crushed. No, the one thing that had truly enabled me to survive the past year, and now these new financial market realities, was the energy, skill, and research of my partner, the other lawyers at our firm, and, especially, the staff. Their work and enthusiasm swirled around me each day, brought my head up, and got my blood moving. It allowed me to expose untruths, to encourage hostile witnesses to tell the truth, to push cases forward, to get results. Over and over, my staff gave more than what was called for by a job. They stayed late. They made copies and filed and stapled and organized before there was any discernible goal or purpose, trusting that somehow the organization I was requesting would allow me to find the answer in a complex case.

So often their efforts paid off. Their work helped me to see the issues within the reams of e-mails and boring closing documents. Every morning, I was greeted by smiles from people who seemed genuinely glad to see me. They waited patiently for my coffee to kick in, for me to start stirring the cases into motion. The discernment of an issue required the assembly of documents, the finding of a witness, the deposition. Once these processes were in motion, I could begin to see how to produce the desired outcome.

The thank-you note project had forced me to see what these people were doing around me. My spreadsheet reflects that I thanked them for gifts and birthday cards, last-minute travel arrangements (tickets appeared based on vague mutterings about plans), for organizing and executing the hurried move of our offices, for rescuing our e-mail accounts and setting up new ones in an afternoon, for volunteering for extra work without being asked when others were out on sick leave, for getting me a new passport and visa for a trip to China in a week, for working on cases so difficult and tedious that I could no longer tolerate them, and for dedicated and uncomplaining hard work that inspired me to stop whining and to work hard every day.

When I started my law practice in 2000, I had been full of the hopes and dreams expressed in my Statement of Ideals. I would deliver legal services of higher quality at lower cost. I would deal fairly and honestly with the courts and the opposing counsel. I would cultivate a happy work atmosphere. In the darkness of 2007, I had failed to notice that I had largely achieved my dream, thanks to the people who were at my side. By Thanksgiving 2008, I saw what they had done and were still doing, and how it had made my dream come true.

A half year had passed since our move to new offices. As legal cases accumulated, so did the file cabinets in the middle of our space. But there was still room left. And on the day before Thanksgiving, the area in front of my desk began to fill with tables and chairs, ham and turkey, cakes and yams, and salad and vegetables assembled by everyone except me. When our office manager had sent the potluck invitation around, I had been too distracted by the latest emergency motion and by the news that I would be working most of the Thanksgiving holiday to respond.

After everyone had gathered for our little party, they grew suddenly quiet. It was one of those silences into which I would ordinarily project a joke. But I didn't, and when someone asked if I wanted to say something, this is what I said: "When we began this year, I made a New Year's resolution that I would try to find one thing each day for which I would be grateful. It is now November. I have kept that resolution. And what I found each day as I searched for someone or something for which to be grateful was that the answer was very often the people I see every morning, who help me through each day, who do the difficult without questioning whether it is necessary, and who look for ways to do more than what is asked. I have learned how truly lucky I am to have in my life the people who are gathered around this table. You have made our firm a good one, and made my life a good one. On Thanksgiving I can truly see at this table how blessed I am and how much I have, how much I should be thankful for."

I could see a smile of sympathy in my paralegal's eyes. Two of the lawyers looked at each other. Then someone asked my partner if she wanted to say anything.

"Not after that," she said.

CHAPTER 20

Running with Friends

During 2007, my supposedly unendurable year, as I whined and obsessed about the problems in my life, my friend Paul, who had been a mentor of mine from my first legal job, an attorney who always remained under consummate and disciplined control, stopped making any sense in the middle of asking a question at a deposition. He had a brain tumor.

After brain surgery and chemotherapy, he had quietly resumed work. But I had not talked to him since I heard the news. I didn't know how to begin the conversation. What should I say: "Is it inoperable?" "How was that surgery?" So I succumbed to insecurity about what to say and did not call.

In 2008, the word got around among Paul's friends that the tumors were back and had spread. He had another surgery, more chemotherapy, and again, things seemed all right. Some months later, however, word got around that there were more tumors. Seven of them.

I needed to overcome my cowardice and get in touch with him. Paul's skill as a lawyer always made me view him as one of the naturals, a man born with an understanding of the role of a lawyer, and a sense of what a lawyer should be doing in a difficult situation. When my own interests were on the line and I had to have a good lawyer, I turned to him. He had seen me through times of weakness and trouble.

I could not let this friend slip away.

Throughout my thank-you note year, when I felt that I had nowhere to turn and didn't know what to do about a situation, I wrote a thank-you note, and that's what I did here. On June 30, I finally had the courage to write to Paul:

I was sure sorry to hear of another tumor. I am praying the chemo will once again do the trick. When I was a young lawyer, you showed me how to do and react to so many things. Now you are setting an example of courage and fortitude that I hope to remember if I am ever faced with a challenge so severe, and I feel once again grateful to know you.

The next day, I got an e-mail: "Thank you for your kind note."

With contact reestablished, I felt I could call and see how Paul was doing. He was willing to talk openly about his disease. The tumors were back and they were growing. Now he needed to find new treatments, because all the normal ones were plainly not working. He was embarking on a series of clinical trials.

Paul explained that he had not changed his life. He continued to work. Sure, you could drop everything and go off on your bucket list, climb a mountain, see the Taj Mahal. Yet while he was doing that, his wife would have to go on with her job as a district attorney. His teenage son would have to go on finishing high school. If he were traveling the world, his family would have to go on without him, all the while thinking of him. They needed to see that his life was going on so that they could feel comfortable going on with theirs. Paul's strategy struck me as so sensible and so right.

Incredibly, one of the ways in which he was going on with his life was to run marathons. Paul liked to run every day, and thirteen miles on Sunday, rain or shine. He wasn't stopping now. He planned to run the Long Beach Marathon in October.

Inspiration came from many sources during this year in my life. Sometimes a voice spoke clearly to me. Sometimes I would find a book behind a chest of drawers or lying on a table in a waiting room. Sometimes the message accumulated. Neil was bugging me. Paul was inspiring me. It was time to try running again.

I tended to eat, watch television, work, and sleep in the small, stifling bubble of space by the laboring old air conditioner in my apartment. Once I put on my new running shoes, however, and ventured out onto Sierra Madre Boulevard, I was reminded of the quaint beauty of Sierra Madre. In my new shoes, I labored slowly past the volunteer fire department and into this charming town. The town has one intersection but no traffic light. Although there is a Domino's and a Starbucks, the local coffee shop and pizza place and even an independent bookstore also survive, along with a series of little shops and a little law office, with legal books in its window that look like they haven't been moved for a generation. I struggled with bad knees, struggled with the emotions brought on by the bank crisis, struggled with obligations to work and family, struggled with the heat in my apartment, struggled to keep on my 365 thank-you notes pace, but I kept jogging.

In early September, Neil came to town to do the Los Angeles Triathlon, as planned. Neil and I had been in regular contact after my thank-you note to him in April. My daughter and I stopped in to see him when I'd had a hearing in his hometown, and Neil had taken us to lunch for a triathlon logistics planning session. I was not going to be ready for a 5K by September, much less a triathlon, so it was agreed that for the Los Angeles Triathlon I would be Neil's support team and official event photographer. I would be in charge of getting him to the start, picking him up at the finish, and making sure he had his equipment and supplies. Neil was solicitous of my daughter, involving her in the conversation at lunch. She loved it.

Los Angeles was sweltering that weekend, and the temperature inside my tiny apartment rose to 100 degrees. The heat soaked into the walls of the building, and the walls radiated through the night, keeping the temperature in the mid-nineties despite the cooling of the Los Angeles evenings. The heat became so intense that it melted the circuits on my daughter's electric piano, causing random keys to play crazily, or not at all.

I began to picture Neil actually in my apartment, and suddenly realized how embarrassing that would be. But the planning had gone too far. He was depending on me, I felt, to provide a place to stay. Determined not to spoil his race by making him attempt sleep in this suffocating heat, I took long sheets of aluminum foil and papered over all the windows to keep out the sun. I think I saw that in a movie about drug addicts who couldn't stand sunlight, but I thought it might help to keep the apartment cool. It helped a little, but not enough. I ran the laboring old air conditioner continuously for two days, but the best I could do was to bring the temperature down to 88 degrees.

Neil was kind enough not to mention the heat in the apartment, and we got to bed early that first night. He claimed he was able to sleep. We got to the start in Venice before dawn, and I said good luck to him as he ran out into the water. Is there anything that looks crazier than hundreds of people rushing into the waves of the cold, dark Pacific Ocean before dawn? I caught Neil staggering out of the ocean after his swim, and he posed briefly for pictures I took with his camera. He was having a good race. I went out to Starbucks.

Later, I took pictures of his confident finish in front of the Staples Center downtown. Except for losing some hair, the main change in Neil since college is that his body is more muscular; he is in better shape now than he was then. He was not the fastest triathlete, but he sure looked incredible. As in college, women were noticing, and I felt like the grayish person in his shadow.

We hung out together for the rest of the day and stayed up late talking that night, even though he had to get on the road back home early in the morning. After Neal took off, my daughter summed up the weekend this way: "You were roommates again." I summed it up in a note:

> *Thanks so much for running in the triathlon down here, and taking the time out to renew our friendship. As I mentioned, I have been so blessed to have lasting and wonderful friends. You've really encouraged me to try to get in shape, and maybe next year we can do one together.*

In the months that followed, Neil and I met for lunch and talked and e-mailed often enough that we felt the friendship completely renewed—closer even than before because now I was Neil's equal rather than the lost little brother I had been in college. We sent books to each other and talked about politics. Neil wrote long, hilarious e-mails, explaining everything I needed to know about cameras (using his camera to photograph him at the triathlon had turned me on to photography), bicycles (as in what I should be riding to get ready for the next triathlon), and women (about which, he assumed correctly, he still knew more than I did). He recommended literary reads; I recommended page-turners. An e-mail on cameras, bicycles, women, or the death penalty would suddenly conclude with a reference to a good book: "Well, I hope you enjoy *Oscar Wao*. I loved it. Keep in touch, my friend."

One day we said the obvious: we had talked more in the last few months than in all of the years since college.

When I'd talked to my friend Paul in early summer and he told me he was running in the Long Beach Marathon in October, I didn't think he would possibly be able to do it. But as the race neared, I checked in with him to see if he would still be running it and he was matter-of-fact. "Of course," he said.

No one in his family found anything very remarkable about this. He was just heading out that Sunday alone like it was any other day. After all, he ran thirteen miles every Sunday. To me it seemed like a world record miracle. He had been on one clinical trial after another all year.

On the morning of the Long Beach Marathon, I walked up and down Ocean Boulevard watching people of all shapes and sizes, alone and in crowds, finishing the marathon. How could so many people manage to do this? I thought.

I was beginning to think I had missed Paul. It had been a couple years since I'd actually seen him; maybe he'd changed so much I hadn't recognized him when he'd run by. But then I did. He was thin. He'd lost some hair, even from his beard.

But he looked fine, running easily and comfortably in the last mile. I ran along with him for a while, talking, got some pictures, and then he was gone.

A week later, Paul and I had dinner with some friends, and I gave Paul the pictures. Paul picked up the tab that night, so I wrote him a thank-you note, which concluded: "Your strength is a great inspiration to me in my much more trivial adversity."

By November, I would be running increasingly long distances with a charity group that raises money to fight leukemia, but before November my progress was slow, so slow as to seem almost like no progress at all. What kept me going? The rekindled friendships with Paul and Neil— and an accident I experienced on the first day I put on my running shoes and went out for a jog.

After running up into Sierra Madre that day, I'd trudged back past my apartment and down the hill into Pasadena. Here, Sierra Madre Boulevard opens up and becomes a proper boulevard with a vast meridian strip. After the Rose Parade each January, the floats sit in this meridian for a few days to allow parade enthusiasts to get a closer look. On my way past the megachurch on the boulevard, I didn't see that the roots of a large tree had disrupted the sidewalk, and I fell. Hard.

After fifty, a fall like this seems different. Without the reaction, balance, strength, and grace of youth, you just go down, filling the distance between the two points with straight, direct motion. It is a shock, like someone hitting you. Your breath is knocked out. And it hurts. This is how falls are going to feel from now on, I thought.

As I got up, I could see three wooden crosses that had been obscured from view by pine and fir trees planted in the grass in front of the church.

I had considered myself something of an atheist for years, but I started going to this church after that fall. The music was plentiful, delivered with professional quality and urgent, genuine enthusiasm. The dominant message was that grace was still available. To everyone. Even to me. I can deal with that, I thought. Through the process of writing thank-you notes, I had developed a notion of being blessed with grace that was meaningful to me. And I could see this grace and these blessings everywhere—in my sons, daughter, siblings, friends, and colleagues, for just a few of more than a hundred examples—where I had not seen it before.

CHAPTER 21

In Training

Beginning in November, every Sunday morning my alarm went off at 5:30 a.m. By 6 a.m., I was driving the Harbor and Santa Monica freeways across Los Angeles to the Santa Monica Civic Center, where I met with a group from the Leukemia & Lymphoma Society's Team in Training. You may see these people running around your town dressed in purple running shirts. I had seen them for years. I had decided to be one of them.

Running with this team would help me get in shape for the Napa Valley Marathon on March 1, 2009. On the way across L.A. every Sunday morning, I listened to *The Jesus*

Christ Show on the radio, the only thing on AM at that hour besides infomercials. There's nothing like being talked to directly by Jesus on AM radio while driving all the way across L.A. in less than thirty minutes as the sun is rising on a Sunday morning. Coming through downtown, you cut across six lanes at the interchange in a few seconds and shoot out onto the Santa Monica freeway, with nothing but empty pavement between you and the ocean, moving at, say, eighty through the space where normally you are slowed to a tedious crawl. The drive was nice, but I was never sure I would make it through the run that would start at the end of the drive. I couldn't believe I was doing this. *Why?*

On one level, I was trying to catch up to the pace of my thank-you project. Having been thrown off by the financial crisis and the breakup with Grace, I was seriously behind on my thank-you notes. Would the thank-you note project be one more failure in my life?

As I thought of ways to pick up my note-writing pace, it occurred to me to do a run for charity. In the nineties I had done a long bike ride, California AIDS Ride 5, from San Francisco to Los Angeles, and then I had run the Marine Corps Marathon for AIDS Project Los Angeles. As I recalled these events, I remembered that many of my friends and business acquaintances had given money to the causes these events supported. These people had deserved the kind of personalized thank-you notes I had begun writing in my thank-you note year, but in those days, I had written form letters. They contained funny and sometimes grandiose accounts of the ride and the run, and they were a kind of thank you, but they were really just form letters. If I did this Team in Training run now, it would give me a good reason to write a lot of thank-you notes, personal ones this time.

I had to try it. The only other way I could think of to get so many more thank-you notes written was to get married again. Without Grace that was not going to happen.

I wasn't just trying to take my mind off a breakup. My resolution to run a marathon in support of the Leukemia & Lymphoma Society had been made four years earlier, when I had briefly considered expanding my practice to include wills and trusts. After buying several thousand dollars' worth of wills and trusts software and books, I had asked a friend to go through the process with me as a trial run. So we sat down together one Saturday and started through the basics of her life. I thought I knew her children and grandchildren.

"So, two children, right?"

She said nothing for a long time. Then, "No, there was a third. I had another son," she said. "He died of leukemia. He was only a teenager."

After she told me that, there was another silence. After a minute or so, I realized she could not go on. I couldn't either. The wills and trusts experiment in my practice was over. I could never open up those books or programs without thinking of my friend's son. I never became a trusts and estates lawyer.

That talk with my friend was often on my mind. I had, from that moment four years earlier, thought of joining the Team in Training people I often saw running around town. I had lost a high school classmate to leukemia. My friend had lost her son. I could not stop being puzzled by how wonderful lives are ended so inexplicably young.

For these years my thought was another unfulfilled resolution. I told myself that I had too much work to do. And after starting my own law firm, I had long given up working out, had gained thirty pounds, and had developed asthma, which left me wheezing at the slightest exertion.

But when I saw my friend Paul run down Ocean Boulevard in October within weeks of finishing his latest round of chemotherapy, my rationalizations seemed lame indeed. I decided I would finally take action and, in the process, finish the thank-you notes.

On the first longish run for Team in Training, as the team headed up San Vicente Boulevard from Ocean Avenue, my wheezing alarmed the program director.

"Do you need to stop? Should we call a doctor?"

"No, it's always like this," I said. "I'm just out of shape."

The image of Paul running to the finish line remained

in my head. I went to Kaiser Permanente, my local clinic, saw my doctor, and got an inhaler. I didn't think of quitting.

The training was exhausting, though, on top of my regular schedule. I would run—well, a more accurate word would be *trudge*—up and down the street in front of my apartment, and afterward I could barely get up the stairs, my knees hurt so badly. Because I was often working late I would not finish the run till ten or eleven. Then I would pile bags of frozen peas and carrots on my aching knees while I ate a frozen pizza.

At first, the Sunday runs were through Santa Monica. Then Santa Monica and Venice. Then Santa Monica, Venice, and Brentwood. Then Santa Monica, Venice, Brentwood, and into Los Angeles. There was camaraderie and cheer on these runs. The sleepy people I ran with each had a story. Most were much younger than I, and many of them had a parent suffering from leukemia or lost to lymphoma. Before or even during the run, runners often shared stories of the loved parent or the lost child. The money being raised by Team in Training did seem to be having an effect. There were many stories of recovery, and of gratitude for a recovery. Some of the runners were themselves in remission.

Gradually, I lost a few pounds. My evening jog went from four to seven miles. My knees felt older than ever, but I was going to finish what I'd started.

The first person to donate to my effort to raise funds

through this run was my friend who had lost her son. "Your support and interest in this project are an inspiration that will keep me running," I wrote in a thank-you note to her.

The training wore me out; I did not have any extra energy to spend on the correspondence asking for money until late in the year. But most of the people I wrote to gave money, and through the marathon, I eventually raised more than $5,000 for the Leukemia & Lymphoma Society. Looking back months later, I saw that I had succeeded because I had used my thank-you note list as the foundation for my mailing list of possible donors. As I wrote to thank each person for opening their hearts and their checkbooks in a time of fear, I realized I had found and identified the generous people in my life, and they did not let me down, even in the midst of a profound financial crisis.

CHAPTER 22

December, the Movie and the Reality; or, It's a Wonderful Life

By December, my life had improved so much I began to imagine a Hollywood ending for the story of my thank-you note project.

While I was catching up steadily to the pace needed to complete 365 thank-you notes, it still looked like I would reach only about 300 notes by the end of the year. But in my imagined happy ending, everything would suddenly come together, just like in the movies.

On Christmas Day, the doorbell would ring, and deliverymen would begin to arrive, from Federal Express, from UPS, from Express Mail. I would stare, dumbstruck, as I began to open the presents. The governor would call, and I would get the judicial appointment I had always wanted. Grace would arrive, saying she wanted to come back to me. After things had quieted down, I would sit and make a list of all the presents and good things that had happened that day. There would be exactly sixty-five things. Just the number of notes I would need to write to finish the project.

What really happened was that I got about the same number of ties and books and shirts as I had received the previous year. I had to work twelve hours on Christmas Day on a pointless motion that my opposing attorney felt was an emergency. Grace did not come back.

Yet, as I began to write my second set of Christmas thank-you notes, I realized that for me, taking stock of what I had, even more than any Hollywood fantasy ending for the year, was proof of the value of the project. Here we were in the midst of the uncertainty of the most difficult economic time since the Great Depression. From what my parents tell me, nobody got Christmas presents during the Great Depression. Yet the people in my life knew I had appreciated what they'd given me last year, and they bought me another gift. And though I had to work on Christmas Day, this was a sign that my business was thriving, something that had hardly been true the previous year. The words in my thank-you notes themselves showed some unbelievable positive changes. In thanking one of the sponsors for my

Team in Training charity runs, I noted that my weekly run in Santa Monica had reached fifteen miles, a distance that would have been absurd for me just a few months before.

If the voice I'd heard in the mountains had implied that I would get all that I wanted, it seemed, at least at this juncture, that it was a promise unfulfilled. Yet, by being thankful for what I had, I realized that I had everything I needed.

Whether or not my life had changed, my experience of it, moment by moment, had been transformed. When bad things happened, they might slow me, but they no longer unraveled me. In looking at the spreadsheet containing the first drafts of my three hundred thank-you notes, I realized that taken together they told a story: even without the Hollywood ending, my year had been a good one.

In my daughter, I had the most precious gift that life can give, a joyful, loving child, willing to learn and to be grateful. She had shown me magic in the tiny apartment where we were living. She taught me how to make even such a humble place better. Through writing thank-you notes, I acknowledged the good things that my ex-wife continued to do for our daughter, which gave me the serenity necessary to move forward to a peaceful end to our marriage. My thank-you notes allowed me to reach out to be thankful for the relationships I had with my other children despite a lifetime of my mistakes.

I had reconnected with friends from college and found

I could still rely on the emotional support of people who had known me for more than thirty-five years. The lawsuit against me had been dismissed. I had found a way to get enough clients to pay their bills and to appreciate those who did. My income had recovered; I was making enough money to support my law practice and my family.

I had not received the judicial appointment I had been looking for, but I had my own law firm, my dear colleagues, and a renewed love for my practice as a lawyer. My life was filled with people who were helping me in large and small ways all day long.

Grace and I had given each other gifts of love throughout the year. We had been grateful for these and recognized their importance in our lives. We gave each other Christmas presents and appreciated the friendship we had, rather than regretted the intimacy we had lost. I was at peace with this relationship, which, unlike others in my past, had ended without bitterness or resentment.

With sixty-five thank-you notes left to go, I had to acknowledge the difficulty of the project. Originally, I viewed this difficulty as arising out of the difficulties of my life. Anyone, I had thought, would have found the exercise a challenge if they had had my problems. Yet three hundred notes disproved this premise. The difficulty of the exercise had been caused not only by external problems but by my own ungrateful focus, my materialistic envy and resentment. At times, these feelings had consumed me. It was little wonder I'd had so much trouble sleeping. During my December 2007 breakfast at that worn-out diner with Bob, I'd told him of my bitterness. I didn't tell him, however, that underneath the bitterness, I had a sense that so many bad things were happening for a reason, and the reason was that I was not a good person. With the help of my three hundred thank-you notes, I had examined the life I had viewed as perfectly awful and found that it was a lot better than I had been willing to acknowledge. Maybe I was not such a bad person after all.

CHAPTER 23

A Better Man

In the first months of 2009, as the March 1 marathon date grew closer, the training for it took over my life. On January 25, 2009, we had to run around the Brentwood Country Club four times, as part of our eighteen-mile run. One of the "mentors" (runners for past events who volunteer their time) ran with me the whole way. On our fourth trip through the Brentwood Country Club, I reached a point of delirium, but he kept me going, in part by pointing out the governor of California, who was out for a walk through the Sunday farmers' market. I wrote him a note:

Thank you so much for hanging with me through the eighteen-mile run. I'm sure my mental health would have taken a turn for the worse at some point without someone to talk to. It was also great fun seeing the Governator. Thanks for pointing him out.

Two weeks later, right before our twenty-mile training run, I got sick. The Sunday runs were crucial to the success of the training, though, and I felt I could not miss even one, so I started the run but, feverish and drenched with sweat, I had to stop at sixteen miles. I wrote a thank-you note to the program director, who drove me back to my car without being grossed out by the fact that every bit of clothing on me was soaked with sweat.

Meanwhile, Paul, one of the first to donate in support of my marathon, had invited me to run a half marathon with him, about thirteen miles, through Palos Verdes, the beautiful coastline neighborhood in southwestern Los Angeles. When we'd made this date, Paul had been uncharacteristically pessimistic. Normal chemotherapy treatments for his new tumors had not worked. There were even more tumors throughout his body, and they were growing. He had tried a few clinical trials without success. His doctors now believed that he had less than a year to live. Reluctantly, he told me, he was thinking of accepting his doctors' advice and quitting work to spend most of his time with his family.

Then, a couple weeks before our scheduled half marathon, Paul had a breakthrough. He wrote me an e-mail with the subject line: "Good news, but will it result in a faster pace?" The latest clinical trial had succeeded against the odds:

My scan results today showed (1) no new tumors, (2) one tumor resolved (gone), and (3) the other 6 to 7 tumors have all decreased to some extent. I will resume infusions next week. Hurray!

Paul was more resolute than ever that we should run this half marathon in Palos Verdes; he reminded me of it several times. So at 5:30 a.m. on a Saturday, I showed up at Point Fermin Park.

It was threatening rain. Paul was bundled in black and looked thinner than he ever had. His voice had a new hoarseness, and he had lost even more hair from the latest chemotherapy. He had been through such an assortment of chemicals that one scarcely knew which round of therapy to blame.

"I'm thinking of running at about two and a half hours. Can you do that?"

"I think so," I said.

I was nervous, even a little scared, about what was to come. I had not been training nearly enough.

About a hundred yards into the race, I fell. Another one of those after-fifty falls where you're on the ground before you know you're falling. My hands got a bit bloody, but I got up and went on.

Then, as we headed down the hill into Palos Verdes, we started to have fun. A muscular man named Steve began to run with us. Steve was a nonstop talker, and he riffed off everyone and everything around him with a hilarious stream-of-consciousness rap that lasted the next two hours. I made the mistake of joking that he could probably get a channel on Sirius to let him provide live commentary for marathons while running them; this seemed to encourage him.

Steve taught at Redondo Union High School. He explained the "Three RUs" he had designed for his students: "First, there's Respect Urself. Of course *yourself* really begins with a *Y* but they get it. Then there's Rise Up. I'm teaching them to stand up for themselves. Then there's Resist the Urge."

I was tempted to ask what urges he wanted the kids to resist (just checking on the status of moral learning in our public schools), but he was too busy explaining how these sayings were going to keep us going for the next ten miles. We were going to resist the urge to fall back. Instead, we were going to rise up, as in up the two- or three-mile hill on the way back. This would cause us to respect ourselves.

We made the mistake of telling Steve our names, which led him to riff on them. He noted that John Paul, when put together, is the name of a recent pope; it is also half the Beatles, and so on. He engaged everyone. He reached out to the police who were watching the intersections. He called out to the people stuck in traffic, waiting for the runners to pass. Some of them were less than pleased by what was going on, but this did not deter Steve.

At about ten miles, we had been going uphill for miles, and I had reached the point where it was no longer a run for fun. I was telling myself to keep up and had been distracted by enjoying both Paul's company and the goofiness of Steve's never-ending raps. Paul sensed that I was starting to labor—the wheezing from my asthma was getting pretty loud—and explained to me that from here on in it was all mental; it was all about whether you could make yourself continue to run despite the pain.

I had no more mental toughness. Everything seemed like pain. I dropped about twenty yards behind Paul as I labored up the last hill. He seemed to be picking up speed.

Then Steve came up next to me and started shouting, literally right in my ear: "Don't give up, John, rise up, baby, you can do it," and so on and so on until finally I shouted back at him: "Okay, for Christ's sake, I'll run faster." And indeed, I picked it up and caught Paul. Now that I was next to him again, I tried to match his tight, economical stride. We were almost there. A picture taken at about this time shows me struggling up the hill with Paul while Steve supervises.

Steve's running became as distracting as his talking. He weaved in and out of the orange cones, as if he were skiing the slalom course. He would pick out a runner up ahead of us—usually an attractive woman—and then he would urge us to run faster so we could catch up to that person. By the end, we were continuing to do this, and as we pulled back into Point Fermin Park, we had run much faster than expected: 2:17. It was exhilarating and fun. For me, this was a pretty good run. For Paul, a fifty-seven-year-old man in the midst of clinical chemotherapy trials, this should be noted as another unique world record.

Over coffee afterward, Paul told me he would be in his latest clinical trial for a year before he would know whether it had succeeded. A year of side effects and fatigue. Already his voice was strained and hoarse, and he seemed a stick-figure drawing of his former self. He admitted that on some mornings, it was hard to get up. Yet, as we sat there in the coffee shop—completely drenched in sweat—we were laughing about the day's run. To be with Paul that day made me feel defiantly alive. I hope he felt that way too. We resolved to run the Long Beach Marathon together in October 2009.

A t 4:30 a.m. on March 1, 2009, telephones rang in every room of a budget hotel in Napa Valley where I was staying with other members of Team in Training. By 5:15 we had boarded school buses that took us twenty-six miles north on the Silverado Trail. As we waited for the 7:00 a.m. start, we huddled in the buses, which kept running and sending out heat. As seven approached, we had no choice but to get out, shield our eyes from the rain to find the start line, listen for the gun, and start running.

The previous night, one of the Team in Training coaches had prepared us for this event by solemnly declaring, "The human body is waterproof." To prove it, he poured a large glass of water over his head. For those of us who did not believe we had the mental power to will away the reality of rain, the team handed out large black garbage bags. Punch three holes for your head and arms, and you have a great disposable rain poncho.

No pep talk is quite enough to make it easy to throw

yourself into the rain with the finish line twenty-six miles away. It does help that thousands of people all around you are doing the same crazy thing. Once on the road, as Paul had counseled me, your mind becomes your main enemy.

As my lungs burned, I thought back to my visit, the previous day, to the Kaiser Permanente booth at the marathon exposition. The booth had a machine into which you would breathe the entire contents of your lungs. It would then provide you with a very official-looking printout telling you the age of your lungs. For most in line in front of me, this had been a confidence builder. All that training had left them with lungs ten or more years younger than they were. My results told me I had the lungs of a sixty-six-year-old man. I don't yet look that old, so the nurse ran the test again. Same result.

"Anything I can do about that?" I asked.

"Well, you'll need to work a little harder tomorrow."

Now, on the road, winding our way through the fog and the rain of the beautiful Napa Valley, I wondered whether this solemn information about my lungs, or my aching back, or some other excuse, would be the one that would cause me to give up. Lots of people give up. I could easily give up.

The first sixteen miles went pretty well. I took it easy, deciding that my goal would be just to beat every novelty runner—you know, the ones with the elaborate costumes and placards that weigh more than they do. I stayed ahead of most of them.

At sixteen miles, though, the fun was over. For me, the twenty-six-mile distance has always seemed insane. On a run that long, the body runs out of ready energy and begins consuming itself, leading one to feel crazily depressed, wanting to cry. Modern running science purports to fix this problem with a variety of newfangled energy goos and candies, but these just leave me nauseated.

What finally got me through on this day were two young men, Raj and Jessie, who were also running for the Leukemia & Lymphoma Society. I watched them for a couple of miles and was impressed by how Jessie, seemingly a much better athlete, kept Raj going and on pace. Finally, I asked to join them, and we became a team. We shared our motivations and talked of the parents or the loved ones who had suffered, or were suffering, from leukemia.

Raj and Jessie were both able to speed up over the last mile. I was a bit delirious and encouraged them to leave me, but they wouldn't, and they pushed me through to the finish line. I tore off the trash bag because I wanted to look good in the pictures. I finished at five hours and nineteen minutes. My shirt looked good in the pictures, even though, like every part of me, it was really, really wet.

Despite the continuous rain, my daughter and her cousins, my ex-wife, and my brother-in-law and sister-in-law were waiting at a point about one hundred yards from the finish line. I told Raj and Jessie to go ahead, and this time they knew I had to hang back for something important. I finished a little slower than they did because I stopped to give my daughter a long, wet hug.

It was the end of the race, but also the end of something bigger. I already suspected then what turned out to be true—that when I wrote my thank-you notes to those who had sponsored me for the run, my project would be complete. The race led me to writing the last of the 365 thank-you notes—and more. I was quickly beyond my goal.

After the marathon, in my hotel room, I did not know whether to get up and walk, as it seemed better just to lie still. My body was getting used to not sweating after five hours of steady sweating. The phone rang. The friend whose son's death had inspired me to do the run was calling. She thanked me for all I had done. I told her funny stories about the day's run, and we chatted about the rain. Then she said something that took me aback, by stating, apropos of nothing in the conversation, "You're a good man, John."

B ack in Los Angeles, I asked Bob, who had paid for that dreadful breakfast in December 2007, if he had noticed any difference in me after 365 thank-you notes.

"A lot," he said. "You are a different and much better person."

Like many lawyers, I had learned to think of myself as an

instinctual expert on people. We believe that within a few seconds we know whether a judge will rule against us, whether a juror will favor our client, whether a witness is lying. Most of all, my assumed people expertise told me people didn't change, and I believed that most of all about the person I thought I knew best of all—myself. I still don't really believe I changed, but the voice let me think that maybe I did, just a little.

So I got what I most wanted.

But I got other things too.

CHAPTER 24

A House, a Dream Job, Grace, and a Sandwich Wrapped in Waxed Paper; or, What I Wanted

This is a video tour of me and my dad and Brody's new house.

My daughter had taken my cell phone. Unlike me, she knew how to use it to take moving pictures. In her video, she is walking through the rooms of our new little house, her hand out in front of her, seemingly talking to herself.

Here's my bathroom. Nice little toilet. Shower. Mirror. Hi, me! This is my room. This is my closet. Pretty nice. Very big.

Soon after the marathon, it became clear I could afford to purchase a small house in the depressed real estate market. The real estate agent had tried to interest me in other houses, but I kept coming back to this cottage near the mountains. The roof was a little crooked over the carport. The dishwasher didn't work. Actually, all of the plumbing was suspect. And there was no air-conditioning. The heating system was broken, and so ancient it could not be repaired. But I could walk directly from the front door onto the path where I had first received my inspiration to write thank-you notes. This was where I needed to be.

At the back of the house there was an extra half room, awkwardly placed between floors, so that you had to jump up, then pull yourself into it. The previous owners had used it as an attic. It was dirty and dusty and had a crack in the ceiling. But I immediately saw it as the successor to my daughter's fort. So did she. By the time she recorded her video tour, the new fort had been carpeted and painted and the crack in the ceiling had nearly been repaired. The fort has a window with a view out to the neighbors' yard. Our new home has a backyard. We transplanted the morning glories and hibiscus flowers we had grown on the little balcony of our old apartment into this yard. Brody now has a chasing-around relationship with Tiger, an older cat who was staying at the house that now belonged to my ex-wife. I once saved Tiger from heart disease and we missed each other. She can live with us now that we have the room.

Here is the legendary crack. Crack, yeah. You can see out the window. We're living next to three dogs. They're wrestling right now.

Here's another mirror. Hi, me, again! Now we're coming outside. Watch your step. Here's a plant that we have. Backyard. Here's some really nice roses. With pink color. Whoa, some dead yellow ones, good yellow ones . . .

My daughter's room has a little cupboard in the wall, where she keeps her favorite rocks and jewelry and pictures. There is also the thank-you note I wrote to her when we were reading *Pollyanna* the year before.

When we moved, the staff at my law firm pitched in to get me a $400 gift certificate to Target, so my daughter and I could go on a shopping spree. In the midst of a world financial crisis, my employees were putting together cash to give a gift to their "boss." I hope that through gratitude, I earned the right to put the word *boss* in quotes. Because that's not the kind of relationship we have.

The previous year, my paralegal, confident in her faith, had assured me that 2008 would be a good year. I did not notice her assurance at the time. I wrote to her individually, though, in thanks for her contribution to our housewarming shopping spree:

> *I wanted to thank you again for participating in the housewarming Target gift certificate. Money is so precious*

these days, and it meant so much to me. My daughter and I went on a shopping spree for her bedroom and playroom and bought a lamp, a chair, pillows, a new comforter set, and some decorations for her bathroom. It was really fun for her, and made her feel like she was having a part in designing her new home.

The fort has evolved. We added a bed for sleepovers. It now functions as a lounge, art studio, and homework room, a clubhouse for a preteen who now calls it "my room-ish."

Okay, I'm signing off now.

One day in July, I was in the midst of an intense settlement conference in the chambers of a federal judge when my cell phone rang. Mortified that I had left it on, I reached into my pocket to shut it off without looking to see who had called.

Only later did I learn that Governor Schwarzenegger's appointments secretary had been trying to reach me. She wanted to know if I could come to Sacramento to meet with her.

I was unable to sleep the night before that meeting. I took an extremely early plane. On the way up, I happened to sit next to the attorney with whom I had carpooled during my first year as a lawyer. I had been nervous after that sleepless night, but this old friend had me laughing.

"Crackers! You're a shoo-in," he said, calling me the name he made up for me when we used to drive together. "They're probably going to announce it next week, and they need to talk to you this week," he assured me. For old time's sake, we shared a cab from the airport. He kept me laughing the whole way, and the remnant of my sleepless night drifted away.

When I met with the governor's appointments secretary, she seemed relatively unconcerned by the issues that had caused unease in earlier interviews, though many new items were also reviewed in a thorough two-hour discussion, including the traffic tickets I got driving my daughter when she was late for school. The governor's appointments secretary was the first person in the judicial application process to notice my law firm's statement of ideals, a source of pride to me, which I had included in my original application, nearly three years earlier.

The next day, I wrote a thank-you note to the old friend who had made me laugh so hard, and I wrote a thank-you note to the appointments secretary:

> *Thank you for meeting with me. You obviously have many factors and applications to consider, so I wanted you to*

know that regardless of the outcome I appreciated the
courteous and thorough inquiry that you made, and the
efforts you made to make it a good experience. I was honored
and privileged to be interviewed.

There was an announcement the following week of a string of new appointments to courts throughout the state. My name was not on the list.

Then, in the first week of September, the governor's appointments secretary called again. There had been a few more judicial vacancies. I had been appointed to the Superior Court.

I wrote another thank-you note to the appointments secretary. I wrote one to Governor Schwarzenegger too.

On the way back from my swearing-in, my daughter again commandeered my cell phone and did a video news report on the event, part of which goes like this:

This is the exclusive interview from Today and Tomorrow. *Here is today's exclusive interview with newest judge John Kralik. Let's see what he has to say.*

"I was very happy, especially because my daughter was there with me."

"Well, let's see, who was it that was holding the Bible?"

"There was some excitement, but I'm pretty sure that was my daughter."

"Well, so now, I have to go. I have to eat lunch, 'cause I actually have a life. That's Today and Tomorrow."

A month before I had been appointed, I had learned of the death of a friend, we'll call him Matthew. Matthew had also briefly been a client, when he asked me to get him released from a hospital where he was held on suicide watch. Feeling obligated in both ways, I went to the service. It was a quiet affair. No one was drinking.

Matthew was a year older than I am. He had died while waiting for a liver. He had not been able to stay sober consistently enough to convince those who give out livers that he truly wanted to live.

Many remembered him that day, the joyfulness, later destroyed by the war in Vietnam, the wicked wit later dulled by substances he used to forget the war. In his darkest moments, he had admitted to some that he didn't want to live. At other moments, he claimed he had not been serious when he said such things. It was said, that day, that in the end he accepted his fate, and the value of his life, as he lay dressed in white, waiting to die. I prayed it was true.

I knew many people at the funeral, but I had managed to sit alone, with an empty seat beside me. Grace had also known Matthew and was there, but I sat in the back, away from her. She was turning around to see who was sitting in the rows behind her. After our eyes met, she came and sat down with me.

One of our friends played guitar and sang Jackson Browne's "For a Dancer," with its sad comment that the purpose of life was unknowable, and revealed itself randomly, if at all. I felt this way about life when I loved that song in college. I might have even felt this way in 2007. But as I sat there, hearing it sung beautifully for my friend, I thought I did not want it sung for me. If there's a reason I'm alive, I want to know.

Maybe because of the Jackson Browne music and our remembrance of the concert, Grace and I hovered so near each other as we walked around after the memorial service and hugged our friend's family that some of our mutual friends thought we had gotten back together. As I said good-bye to her that night I said, "It was nice that we could be together tonight."

"It was nice for me too," she said. We agreed to meet for lunch.

After our lunch, when we walked out from the restaurant, our shoulders were close. She took my arm. She hung on. I let her.

When I brought up that first night when she left me

and walked up the driveway alone, she explained: "It wasn't that I didn't want a Christmas present. It's just that what I really wanted was you."

Our first real date was the September Dodgers playoff game against the Phillies, the only one the Dodgers would win. Below our cool loge-level seats, the team owners, Frank and Jamie McCourt, circled each other warily in the heat of the owners' box, divorce lawyers and Kobe Bryant among their famous guests. It was the average Los Angeles celebrity pageant: humanity on display in a way that made you feel simultaneous sympathy and envy.

Two rows down from us though, an anonymous elderly couple watched the game, their shoulders gently touching. They had eschewed the $5 Dodger dogs and the $10 beers. Instead, the wife reached into her purse and withdrew a sandwich, lovingly wrapped in waxed paper. Though we could have been watching the game, or the unfolding drama in the owners' box, Grace and I were instead transfixed by the unfolding of this waxed paper. We turned to each other as we realized that we had both been watching the gentle hands of this elderly lady unfolding the waxed paper, taking out the sandwich, and offering it to her husband. Then she adjusted the collar of his white cotton shirt, smoothed a few lumps in his thin gray hair, and whisked away a couple ticks of dandruff.

"Waxed paper," we said to each other. "Who does that anymore?" Everyone just throws a sandwich into a Ziploc bag. Within a week, both of us had bought rolls of waxed paper. I now wrap my daughter's sandwiches in it. If Grace stops by for lunch, she has wrapped our sandwiches in it.

How and why and whether Grace will stay is a story for another day. I am grateful for what I have.

You can give your love a nice house on the beach, or a Lexus, or even something bigger, but it won't beat a sandwich wrapped in waxed paper. Or a thank-you note. "Who does that anymore?"

A Tie

My own responses to the search for thank-you note topics and the reactions of those to whom the notes were written kept me writing them from January 3, 2008, through the fifteen months it took me to finish the 365 thank-you note project and beyond. Because this process has turned my life around, and continues to do so to this moment, I have not stopped writing these notes.

Neither have I stopped keeping up my spreadsheet. If I am ever upset or disgusted with life, I look at my spreadsheet to see when I wrote my last thank-you note. Usually, I find it has been too long. In fact, that happened today while I was writing this account.

Because of my spreadsheet, I can look back and find notes like these:

Dear Daughter:

Thank you so much for the brown tie with the blue spots. It is just the kind of tie I like and it goes with my tan and my blue suits.

It was fun to be with you over Christmas and New Year's.

Love,
Dad

When I put on this tie today, I remember it was the gift that most brightened the end of my worst year. I wear it often.

How to Write
Thank-You Notes

I knew at some point I would need to do some research on the proper way to write a thank-you note. So I thought I would write out my own notions of thank-you note writing at the beginning, before they were colored by the formulas of conventional wisdom.

A couple things were clear to me from the get-go. You ought to mention the gift itself, hopefully in a positive tone, just to prove you know what it is and aren't confusing the gift giver with someone else. Then maybe a sentence or two explaining how the gift is changing your life—if anything plausible could be said in that regard. Then maybe there is something you had forgotten to thank the person for in the past, or you could mention the importance of his or her friendship.

Many of my notes were not about material gifts. In these notes, I tried to describe just what the other person had done for me and to show my understanding of that person's effort. I started to recognize that people were doing things because they cared and to praise that care for what it was— a rare vestige of human goodness. I tried to show an understanding of their special nature and effort. This was part of my shift of focus from the gift to the giver.

If the recipient had a sense of humor, I thought, perhaps I might try to end with some attempt at humor. I was very uncertain as to that tactic. If the joke fell flat, you had to start a new note. I used small three-by-five cards: there was no space for a setup to get the tone right. I didn't want to use a big card because the exercise was not to write thank-you letters, just thank-you notes. I decided that, for the most part, humor was not going to work for me.

The brevity of a small card isolates your gratitude from your other more complex, and less admirable, thoughts. Unlike the potential boundlessness of e-mail, there is no room for qualification, for responding to every other aspect of that person's recent behavior and communications. There is only room to focus on the one good thing that person just did for you, and your gratitude for that one good thing. For this one moment and this one communication, all else is left aside.

To learn more, above and beyond my initial notions of note writing, I borrowed some old etiquette books from Grace's mother. I started with *Emily Post on Etiquette,* which, as of 1987, the date of the paperback I was reading, was being updated by Emily's granddaughter-in-law, Elizabeth, Emily apparently having passed on in 1960.* The book lists occasions when thank-you notes are mandatory, including Christmas and birthday gifts, and even personal messages. I estimated that I had sent thank-you notes about .1 percent of the time for such gifts. Well, at least I was doing better for Christmases after 2007.

Writing 365 thank-you notes in fifteen months was a stretch—and forced me to look at the many things in my life for which I needed to be grateful. Looking back at the list, however, I see now that at least a hundred of these were notes I should have been writing all along for Christmas presents, housewarming gifts, extraordinary efforts by my coworkers, special gifts from friends, concert and sports tickets, dinners and expensive lunches. In a year in which there was a special event or wedding or other event that could require a hundred or so notes all by itself, I might have 365 notes that should be written just to recognize all the good stuff in my life. During the remainder of 2009, I wrote another hundred notes. Looking back at the list of thank-you notes, I think that many Americans could easily write one hundred thank-you notes per year.

This may seem daunting, but perhaps start by replacing all your thank-you e-mails with handwritten thank-you notes.

---

* Elizabeth L. Post, *Emily Post on Etiquette* (New York: Harper & Row, 1987).

The notes that came to me reinforced my conviction that handwriting is important and special, that it forces a concentration on the task. I continue to believe that the best thank-you notes are handwritten. It is what sets a thank-you note apart from an e-mail. I, for one, was just using plain note cards, so I know that there was nothing about the cards themselves that was special; there was nothing that distracted from the message.

Even in business, a handwritten note still plays an important role. It doesn't take a lot more time or effort than writing an e-mail, which inevitably is buried in the annoyance of a glowing screen and promptly lost in cyberspace. A handwritten note just feels like sincere gratitude. It conveys your physical presence to the receiver. You are right there, not far away at the other end of a machine. Even when it's just business, people feel it, and they respond.

I'm not saying you should not use e-mails to say thank you. I wrote or received more than one thousand e-mails in 2008 that contained the words *thank you.*

As another general rule, I intuitively seemed to know that one shouldn't get into a story of an exchange or of regifting in the thank-you note. This was confirmed by research: "Do not ask where the gift was purchased so that you can exchange it."* If the friend is close enough, they will let you

---

* Rosalie Maggio, *How to Say It* (New York: Prentice Hall, 1990), p. 344.

know. Otherwise, you can get value out of any gift, if only by donating it to charity.

Books on thank-you notes filled my head with phrases of cheerful praise and gratitude, as in "I can't remember when I've had a better/more pleasant/more relaxing/more enjoyable time."* Viewing these phrases, I thought I could develop a computer program that would draft the perfect thank-you note.

Even so, I decided to write, as well as I could, from my heart.

As with all writing, thank-you notes improve if you revise them. For me, my spreadsheet gave me the opportunity to do a first draft. So when I picked up the pen, I was rewriting. I was less apt to run out of space on the small card, less likely to put the sentences out of order. Less likely to decide what I was saying was too awkward. I recommend one rewrite to make sure your sentiment is conveyed clearly and honestly.

The best thank-you notes will stir in the recipients' hearts the knowledge that their gesture was truly appreciated, and even inspire the desire to give again, knowing that they will be thanked and appreciated.

The one sure piece of advice I have on how to write thank-you notes is this: write a lot of them. Many of the notes I wrote at the beginning of the year provoked the biggest

---

* Maggio, *How to Say It*, p. 350.

reaction because people were, frankly, in shock that I had written them. Some of the notes later in the year were more apt, got directly to the heart of what I wanted to say to my correspondents, and showed that I could sincerely appreciate and understand them and their efforts. There was, occasionally, a certain eloquence to them. One quasi-scientific measure of this improvement is that when I ran a second marathon for the Leukemia & Lymphoma Society, most of my donors gave again, despite the deepening of the recession in the meantime. I was really much better after writing about 100 notes than I was before I wrote them. After writing 365 thank-you notes, I was getting good at it.

I did not view writing thank-you notes as a self-help system, nor did I view it as a new, positive psychological method to delude myself into believing that my life is better than it really is or to cultivate an artificial state of well-being. This is just an exercise in average good manners. I was simply engaging in a custom my grandfather had attempted to teach me nearly fifty years ago.

At the risk of making an unscientific and directly moral statement, I will say that writing thank-you notes is a good thing to do and makes the world a better place. It also made me a better man. More than success or material achievement, this is what I sought.

I still owe my grandfather that second thank-you note.

A Statement of Ideals

This is the statement of ideals I posted on the wall of my law firm when I began it in 2000.

A Statement of Ideals

To clients:

We will strive
- To price services substantially less than competitors for the same amount and quality of service.
- To provide clients with correct legal advice.
- To communicate with clients honestly, and in

clear, understandable language. All phone calls and e-mails are to be returned within 24 hours, or there will be no charge.

- To work diligently for clients using the best talents of intellect, hard work, and creativity, while abstaining from tactics of annoyance, embarrassment, diversion, and delay.

To ourselves:

- We will be committed to the success and personal well-being of every single person employed by the law firm. We will not allow work to destroy our ability to have a full, productive, and loving life outside of the office.
- We will seek to train less experienced lawyers, paralegals, and assistants—even if training time cannot be fairly billed to clients.
- We will seek to fairly compensate each individual according to that person's proportionate contribution to the success of the firm.
- We will not fail to represent clients whose legal and factual positions are defensible merely because they are unpopular, politically incorrect, or even shunned by others. Nevertheless, we will be true to our beliefs in right and

wrong, both as lawyers and as human beings. If our principles conflict so fundamentally with those of the client that we cannot provide the client with the best possible representation, we will seek to withdraw promptly from the representation on terms that fully protect the client's rights.

To the Courts:

- We will represent our clients with respect for the integrity of the legal system.
- We will not mislead the Court as to any matter of fact or law.
- We will not fear to inform the Court that it is in error.

To our colleagues and opposing counsel:

- We will compete against you fairly, and with respect.
- We will also work with you to find solutions to legal disputes that are fair and satisfactory to all concerned.
- We will work together with all lawyers to advance the integrity and ideals of the profession.

To our community:

- We will donate at least 5 percent of our profits or our time to the community.

Finally, we are human. We can make mistakes, or have bad days. But every person in this law firm pledges to do our best in living up to this commitment.

When you retain us, we ask you to help us live up to this pledge.

Although I am gone from the firm, this statement is still there on the wall outside my old office.

Acknowledgments

The heroes of my story are the more than four hundred people to whom I have written thank-you notes over the last two years. At each stage of the project, their reactions, and their return to me of spiritual, loving, and material "silver dollars," kept me going, wanting to see what would happen next. They keep me writing thank-you notes today.

My heroes include my children; my parents; my brothers and sisters; my former spouses; my in-laws; my friends who listened to and understood me; my office manager; my partners; my associates; my paralegals; the professionals who interpreted, reported, consulted, and mediated in my cases; the attorneys who referred cases; opposing attorneys who settled cases; the court clerks who patiently dealt with me;

my doctors and dentists, who cared for me; the teachers and doctors who cared for my children; my clients who paid me and otherwise appreciated my work; the people who waited on me, found and returned things to me, fixed and cleaned my apartment, gave money to my charitable causes, fixed my computers and autos, moved my home and office, cut my hair, provided suits and advice to me, served me coffee, taught me, watched my cats, drove me to the airport, did my laundry, listened to me, and inspired me; and those who picked up the tab at breakfast, lunch, and dinner; gave me Christmas and birthday presents; taught me; mentored me; inspired me; interviewed me; and appointed me. And loved me—thank you again, Grace.

The voice that originally insisted I write 365 thank-you notes then insisted on priority again. Until I could write something about the 365 thank-you notes, there would be no other writing. So I began to compile this book. It seemed odd to write again. I had given up any dreams of being a writer when I went to law school. My early attempts to write were kept in that box I never looked in. I kept it tucked away, out of sight, so I wouldn't be reminded of this lost dream. But even when I left everything else behind, I had taken it with me. I still couldn't bear to read the stories and relive the pain, but I finally opened the box to connect to the past I had given up.

Unlike my previous attempts at writing, which always seemed to founder, this one seemed to flow; this one had a life of its own. Originally, I saw it as something cute, a cheery book about how to write thank-you notes. Then, just as when Samuel Richardson wrote *Pamela; or, Virtue Rewarded*, the letters began to tell a story. And those who read it first told me the story had a beginning, a middle, and an end, if I could find them.

By December 2009, I had finished a draft of the book and thought of beginning to seek an agent or publisher. At 7:19 a.m. on December 14, 2009, I sent out an inquiry letter through an Internet service that queries agents and publishers. Then the ending I hoped for in December 2008 began happening.

My first favorable response was received at 7:22 a.m. I checked my e-mail at about 9:00 a.m., not realizing that the inquiry letter had gone out. There were dozens of favorable responses, saying things like:

What a lovely journey!

I love this idea, and think it's an exercise everyone should do.

An editor at a university press wrote:

> A great idea, and I might try this myself! You should
> get an agent. Try Marly Rusoff.

At 8:27 a.m., Marly herself wrote:

> Please do send me what you have. It sounds like a
> great project.

In a panic, I called a friend of mine who is a writer and
started reading off the names of the agents and publishers
who wanted to see the manuscript.

"Are any of these real?" I asked.

"They all are," he said, after I had read him the names.
"What, exactly, was your idea?"

Given that I knew nothing about publishing, it is astonishing that I was able to choose Marly Rusoff a few days
later. She proved to be a rare find, an agent who valued and
cared about me more than a possible sale.

Soon Marly found Hyperion, Ellen Archer, and Barbara

Jones. As my editor, Barbara had the difficult task of working with a first-time author to change the manuscript into something that could be accessed and read with interest. Working with a first-time author on a book he never expected to write must be a peculiar challenge, and Barbara always made it fun and stimulating.

While this is a true story, some of the names and identifying details of the persons involved have been changed. I did not keep the thank-you notes themselves, only a first draft in my spreadsheet. So the actual notes may be a little different than the words quoted here. I hope some are better in the second draft. Some events did not occur in the precise order or at the precise time related in the book. As with any writing, this story reflects only my perspective on events, and, as the book relates, my perspective became more balanced as the project went on. I do not mean to hurt or judge the others who are depicted in this book, especially because I am grateful to all of them for their role in this journey. Because the book needed to be accessible to a broad audience, many who made huge contributions to my life and well-being are mentioned only briefly, or not at all. Even after five hundred notes, there are many whom I still haven't thanked.

When I dare to hope that others will read this, I do not have the illusion that I found the perfect agent within sixty-eight minutes, and the perfect editor and publisher within a month, solely as the result of my skill as a writer— a talent that somehow went unused and undiscovered for decades. Rather, I can only surmise that the voice I heard in the mountains on January 1, 2008, was seeking a broader audience, and knew how to get it.